The Sermon on the Mount

Studies and Sermons

Kerygma and Church

The Sermon on the Mount

Studies and Sermons

Scott Nash

Editor

ISBN 1–880837–06–4

Contents

Preface to the Series

Smyth and Helwys Publishing presents the *Kerygma and Church* series in the hope of filling a void in literature available to ministers and churches. In particular, the series seeks to bridge the gulf too often separating the study from the pew and the academic classroom from the context of church life. The series legitimates its existence by the conviction that biblical scholarship has significant and relevant contributions to make to the ongoing life of the community of faith.

Because of its stated aim to connect the serious study of the Bible with the life of the church, the series intends to feature the contributions of persons who themselves are sensitive to the relationship between scholarship and church life. Whether the approach be primarily exegetical or expository, a sensitivity to both endeavors should be evident.

Both academicians and ministers/church leaders will find an avenue here to articulate their understandings of the Kerygma. The series further aims to be inclusive of the diversity within the total body of believers. While the series is expressly by Baptists and for Baptists, an inclusive spirit will also at times lead us to consider other perspectives.

As students of baptist history would expect from any endeavor invoking the revered names of (John) Smyth and (Thomas) Helwys, freedom of inquiry and expression is paramount for this series. A respect for scripture as authoritative religious literature bearing the Kerygma of the Word of God directs scholarship to listen carefully to what is said in order to learn how to respond faithfully. Beyond this healthy concern to "hear and obey," however, no other parameters are permitted to dictate the direction of study or the application of its findings. Through exegesis and exposition of biblical texts, the works of this series will strive to connect the Kerygma of God with the Church of God.

The Editors
Greenville, SC

Preface

The present volume is designed to stimulate the act of listening to the Sermon on the Mount by providing a mixture of exegetical, thematic, and homiletical approaches to the text. A deliberate effort to present diverse Baptist perspectives has been a guiding aim in constructing the book. Some of the studies deal with technical matters of exegesis, while other chapters focus more on practical application. Some studies tease the mind, while others touch the heart. Some chapters reflect the seasoned perpsectives of a senior generation of scholars and preachers. Others represent the insights of younger students of the sermon. American, National, and Southern Baptist views are joined together here, as are those who approach the text from the vantage point of being female or male, white or African-American, southern or northern.

The significance of Jesus' relationship to the Jewish law is apparent in the number of studies and sermons that draw from Matthew 5. The inclusion of several treatments of the same passages by different persons is deliberate; the words of the Sermon on the Mount cannot be bound by any one (or anyone's) interpretation.

Any work on the Sermon on the Mount is best undertaken in a spirit of humility. The text itself speaks powerfully enough to humble any interpreter, not to mention the humility that comes from the many debts one incurs along the way. I must mention some of those to whom I am indebted.

Gordon Windsor (Centre College) first and Frank Stagg (Southern Seminary) foremost opened up the text of the Sermon for me and seduced me to further study. I've learned much from T. C. Smith and W. Clyde Tilley as I edited the copy for their own books on the Sermon on the Mount. The chapter in this volume by T. C. Smith is based on the same original paper which underlies the second chapter of his book on the Sermon on the Mount; I thank him for letting me use the material in a different way here. I am indebted to each of those who contributed to this volume. Their efforts enriched my own understanding, and I thank them all.

I gratefully acknowledge the permission granted by Kay Weiner of Koinonia Partners to use Clarence Jordan's Cotton Patch Version here. James Pitts first suggested that I include Jordan's translation and provided a copy of it. I also thank Cecil Staton for his assistance in this project and for his vision for Smyth & Helwys. Thanks go to Ron Jackson for his work on the cover design and his attention to other matters. Edd Rowell of Mercer Press generously provided much technical advice. Jamie Thomas, my student secretary at Brewton-Parker College, typed much of the material onto computer disk.

I thank Dawn, my wife, and Marc and Chris, my sons, for their support and patience during the chaos that has reigned in our household since the birth of Smyth & Helwys.

Scott Nash
Ailey, Georgia
1992

Introduction

by Scott Nash

The words of the Sermon on the Mount are penetrating words. At times they are simultaneously disturbing and comforting, frustrating and invigorating, indicting and redeeming. Few passages evoke such mixed reactions of dread and awe as the simple, yet at times outrageous, teachings of Jesus in the Sermon on the Mount.

As is true of other portions of Scripture that probe the deepest veins of human existence, the Sermon on the Mount has had more distant admirers than close friends. While many have considered its teachings to be beautiful ideals that repeatedly challenge persons to their most noble efforts, only a few have heard these same teachings as a compelling call to a particular way of life. Fewer still have dared to heed the call.

Interpretations of the Sermon on the Mount

1. Early Church Assessments

The early recognition of the importance of the Sermon on the Mount, as well the acknowledgement of the difficulty of interpreting and applying its teachings, is evident in the writings that have survived from the days of the early church. Before the Council of Nicea in 325 CE, Christian writers cited the Sermon on the Mount more than any other section of the Bible.[1] They and their opponents viewed the teachings of Jesus included there as prescriptions for living that were to be strictly obeyed. They also recognized that obeying them was not an easy matter. After Nicea, the triumph of Christianity in the Roman empire greatly increased the church's numbers, though not necessarily enlarging the number of persons committed to its teachings since many had been incorporated into the church through mass conversions.

2. Medieval Scholasticism

While being a Christian had previously in itself involved a certain separation from the world, the rise of a society often only formally Christian led many devout Christians to withdraw from society altogether or in part in order to practice the more ascetic kind of life they saw required by Jesus' words. Monasticism was born, and along with it came a divided church. Only a select few, such as the monks, could give themselves completely to following the teachings of Jesus; the rest could settle for obedience to the minimal requirements for salvation. The great medieval theologian Thomas Aquinas and other church scholars distinguished between the *praecepta* ("precepts") that were binding on all Christians and the *consilia* ("evangelical counsels") that were to be followed by those pursuing greater righteousness and perfection.[2] The teachings of the Sermon on the Mount, demanding as they are, were considered *consilia*.

3. Reformation Reappraisals

The Reformation saw the rise of two very different approaches to the Sermon on the Mount. On the one hand, leading reformers such as Martin Luther and John Calvin rejected the idea that the ethical imperatives of the Sermon on the Mount were intended for only the spiritually elite within the church. Luther held that the Sermon's teachings were binding on all Christians. He further held, however, that one had to distinguish between one's role in the world and one's citizenship in the kingdom of Christ.[3] As a "person" in the kingdom of Christ, the Christian was bound to live in accordance with the Sermon on the Mount. But because of one's "office" within the worldly kingdom, the Christian must realize that limitations exist for living out the Sermon's teachings in the secular realm.

This Two-Kingdoms approach enabled him to emphasize that the ideals of the Sermon served to indict humankind in its sinfulness. In this, he was echoing the Pauline and Augustinian view about the limited positive function of the law and the necessity of grace. Luther held that the Beatitudes, however, also pointed the way toward the salvation God had provided through Christ despite the inevitable inability of Christians to transport their heavenly obligations fully into the earthly realm.

Calvin's approach was to affirm the applicability of the Sermon to all Christians while insisting that its demands must be viewed in the light of the total witness of Scripture.[4] In contrast to the Scholastic theologians, he argued that the Sermon's commands—when properly read through the lens of the rest of Scripture—did not constitute binding legalism but rather opened one to the true and binding "spirit" of the law.

The Pauline-Augustinian-Lutheran emphasis on the necessity of grace for a sinful humanity—whose wretched condition receives further exposure and indictment from the perfectionism called for in the Sermon on the Mount—can be detected more recently in the significant approach of Eduard Thurneysen.[5] The Sermon on the Mount, in his view, is the place where the living word of Christ confronts us both as demand and grace. The demand of the Sermon is fulfilled only in the death and resurrection of Christ. Jesus himself fulfills the law he commands in the Sermon. Because the

Sermon on the Mount cannot be separated from the rest of the gospel story, Thurneysen held that it is fundamentally a word of grace to us.

4. Radical Applications

The Reformation's elevation of the authority of the Bible led some radical groups to contend for an extremely literalistic interpretation and application of its teachings, especially the demands of the Sermon on the Mount. The Anabaptists, in particular, argued that the Sermon's ideals were to be practiced by all Christians in every realm of life.[6] To do this, they sometimes sought to take over the reigns of government and enforce the transformation of society or, when failing this, to withdraw from the decadent society and form their own communities structured according to the new law of the gospel.

While the radical groups were less successful in the long run than the major reformers (except for the few who did establish continuing communities such as the Mennonites), their perspective has reappeared periodically in significant figures. The Russian writer Leo Tolstoy, for example, argued that the Sermon's teachings were to be accepted and applied just as they read.[7] In particular, Christians should not become angry (for any cause), divorce (for any reason), take an oath, or resist evil, and should love their enemies (even enemies of their nation). His advocacy of absolute nonresistance has received the most attention (and criticism) and has continued to influence those working for peace in the modern era, including Gandhi and Martin Luther King, Jr.

5. Ethical Re-orientation

The difficulty of achieving a consensus about whether one should seek to obey the ethical imperatives of the Sermon on the Mount in a strict fashion—in addition to the problem of actually doing so should one decide that is what is required—has led many interpreters to see them more as an appeal to conscience than as a call for specific action. Wilhelm Hermann, a professor of systematic theology at the University of Marburg and teacher of such notable scholars as Karl Barth, Martin Dibelius, and Rudolf Bultmann, asserted that the Sermon's demands were both unattainable and invaluable for humanity.[8] One should see them not as commands but as illustrations of what life guided by genuine love for a sovereign God and love for the neighbor is like.

Bultmann differed from his teacher, Hermann, in seeing the demands of Jesus in the Sermon on the Mount in terms of a call for radical obedience.[9] What is required is more than the performance of particular actions or the adoption of a particular attitude. What is required is a decision of total obedience of the whole self to the call of God in Christ. What this means in terms of specific action is not spelled out—indeed, it cannot be, according to Bultmann.[10] Günther Bornkamm has carried this perspective further in asserting that the Sermon makes a radical claim on persons to orient their whole existence toward the eschatological vision of the kingdom of God seen in Jesus and to work in this world to establish signs of that kingdom.[11]

6. Historically Conditioned

The rise of historical criticism has led many New Testament scholars to insist that the Sermon on the Mount be viewed from the perspective of its historical context. This approach has actually focused on two contexts: (1) the life setting of Jesus as a way of understanding the Sermon's original intent and (2) the setting and purpose of the author of the Gospel of Matthew in which the Sermon appears. The first concern coincided with the rise of the quest for the historical Jesus, while the second is more a result of redaction criticism's attempts to identify the theological agendas of the Gospel writers.

(1) The Life Setting of Jesus

At the end of the nineteenth century a movement known as the history of religion school was dominant in German biblical scholarship.[12] Scholars such as Wilhelm Boussett and Wilhelm Heitzmüller argued that Jesus and the movement stemming from him had to be viewed against the background of the numerous religious groups existing in his time. They held that Judaism existed in many forms (a view that has been confirmed by more recent study) and that both Judaism and Christianity were influenced by other currents operative in the larger Greco-Roman world.

Johannes Weiss located Jesus' perspective within the context of a form of Judaism highly affected by apocalyptic expectations regarding the coming of the messiah and the end of the world.[13] He held that Jesus believed in an imminent arrival of the kingdom of God and was therefore calling his disciples to live in accordance with that coming kingdom. Albert Schweitzer considered Jesus' demands in the Sermon on the Mount to be an "interim ethic" designed to separate his followers from all worldly standards in preparation for the kingdom's arrival—which Jesus fully expected during his lifetime.[14] Since the kingdom did not come, Schweitzer held, the Sermon on the Mount cannot be seen as a guide for living that is to be strictly followed by Christians. In his own life, however, Schweitzer sought to live according to its basic principles.

C. I. Scofield drew strangely similar conclusions about the practicability of the Sermon on the Mount, but he drew them from a very different reading of the eschatological dimension of Jesus' teachings.[15] He held that the Sermon on the Mount was always only intended to be followed during that dispensation when the kingdom of God had arrived in fullness. He asserted that Jesus never intended for his disciples or for Christians before the end-time to live according to the Sermon on the Mount, though they might receive some benefit from its principles.

A more thoroughgoing denial of the Sermon on the Mount's relevance for contemporary Christians came from Friedrich Naumann.[16] While at one point in his life he believed that Jesus' teachings provided the basis for a Christian economic and political order, a trip to Palestine convinced him otherwise. Seeing the continuing poverty and primitive conditions of that land, he concluded that Jesus' ethical demands were not only impractical for modern times but also inappropriate for Jesus' own day. Jesus had been too bound by his rural Jewish culture and could not adequately address the changing economic situation in a way that would prepare his followers to work for better conditions.

Hans Windisch countered those who stressed the eschatological orientation of Jesus' teachings.[17] He conducted a thorough historical analysis of the Sermon on the Mount and concluded that eschatology was not the dominant perspective of Jesus or Matthew. The Sermon on the Mount stands more in the tradition of the prophetic and wisdom movements of the Old Testament, he asserted. Jesus (and Matthew) saw his words as a completion of the Jewish law, and he expected his followers to fulfill the law by obeying his commands as a means to salvation. Jesus' perspective differed from that of Paul and the early church which saw Jesus' death and resurrection as the basis for salvation. Nevertheless, Windisch saw in the Beatitudes a word of grace that gave hope beyond the law for the "poor in spirit," those who would acknowledge their inability to will or to achieve obedience to Jesus' commands and who had to trust in God's promise to deliver.

Arguing that the Sermon on the Mount is best understood in the context of rabbinic Judaism, Paul Billerbeck and Gerhard Kittel held that no particular teaching of the Sermon on the Mount is unique to Jesus.[18] His ideas can all be found in some form in the teachings of the rabbis contained in the Talmud (which was codified in its final forms centuries after Jesus). What is unique to Jesus, Kittel asserted, is the way he exaggerated his ethical claims to demonstrate humanity's total inability to fulfill righteousness and absolute need for the saving work of God in Christ.

These and other attempts to understand Jesus within the context of his own history led many scholars to conclude that the Sermon on the Mount could not function as a guide for specific action or even as a basic orientation for one's attitude in regard to God and the world. The closer these scholars believed they were getting to the historical Jesus, the more alien and irrelevant the Sermon on the Mount seemed to become.

(2) The Life Setting of Matthew

Since the time of Windisch's study (the first German edition was published in 1929), historical analysis has dominated the efforts of New Testament scholars who have turned their attention to the Sermon on the Mount. Source critical and redactional analyses have led many to see the Sermon as primarily the product of the author of Matthew. While many factors have contributed to the rise of this view, a basic support comes from the comparative study of Matthew and Luke. Many of the same teachings that appear in the Sermon on the Mount are also found scattered throughout Luke's Gospel. This suggests that at least one of the evangelists has deliberately organized the teachings ascribed to Jesus in ways that support the particular portrait of Jesus being presented. Since the pattern of clustering Jesus' teachings together appears in several sections of Matthew, many conclude that the same holds for the Sermon on the Mount. Recognizing this helps one gain perspective on the specific message Matthew wished to convey. (See the comparison of Matthew and Luke below.)

W. D. Davies has conducted the most exhaustive historical analysis to date of the setting of the Sermon on the Mount.[19] Focusing on the setting of the Sermon within the Gospel of Matthew, he has concluded that the Sermon on the Mount can only be understood against the background of the development of rabbinic Judaism after the fall of Jerusalem in 70 CE. Certain Christian groups found themselves competing with the authority of the rabbis of Jamnia who were formulating new torah (instruction pertaining to the law of Moses). Additionally, other groups of Jews espoused expectations of a messianic figure other than Jesus. Matthew used the Sermon on the Mount and other materials to present Jesus as a "new Moses" who came as the Messiah and gave the authoritative interpretation of the old law.

Georg Strecker has arrived at similar conclusions.[20] According to him, Matthew took traditions that rooted in Jesus' own ministry, but which had passed through several stages of development, and constructed a sermon that clearly revealed Jesus as the son of God. The one whom the church knew as its resurrected and exalted Lord—and for whom it had been waiting in vain to return—was shown to be the same Jesus who called them to a greater righteousness. Matthew intended for this call to righteousness to be binding upon his readers as they struggled to live out the kingdom vision while awaiting its delayed arrival.

Following an approach that focuses more on the literary features of the Sermon on the Mount, Hans Dieter Betz has identified what he holds is the literary genre of the Sermon.[21] The Sermon on the Mount follows the pattern of the "philosophical epitome," a type of writing used in antiquity to give a synopsis of a larger body of teaching. This allowed persons who did not have access to the whole body of teaching to apply its principles in particular contexts. Betz holds that Matthew received the Sermon from a Jewish Christian group that had developed it to counter the claims of Judaism and the anti-legalism of certain gentile churches. The Sermon on the Mount demonstrated that Jesus was an orthodox Jew who demanded obedience to the written torah as a necessary requirement for entrance into the kingdom. The Sermon further showed this Jewish Christian group how they were to understand and apply the torah in order to attain a greater righteousness.

John P. Meier and Robert A. Guelich, in separate studies, have argued that the Sermon on the Mount was part of Matthew's total effort to demonstrate that Jesus had transcended the torah altogether.[22] The Sermon calls for a greater righteousness than what can be obtained through the law— one grounded in the ministry of Jesus who announced the arrival of God's kingdom and, through illustrations of righteous behavior, required followers to live lives befitting kingdom existence.

The various approaches to the interpretation of the Sermon on the Mount indicate that no one has yet found a completely adequate way to understand its message and its significance for living. Studies show that the Sermon on the Mount can and must be viewed from many different angles. The historical backgrounds of both Jesus and the Gospel's author must be considered in order to understand basic concepts and images. For this reason, the context of first century Judaism in all of its diversity must be examined apart from the misconceptions that have grown from the misreading of that context and have led to much misunderstanding about Judaism and the role of the torah (law) within it. In addition, the Sermon on the Mount cannot be studied in isolation from its setting in the Gospel in which it appears. The Sermon is a part of a larger literary whole—a Gospel that has its own distinctive message about Jesus and what it means to follow him.

The literary context of the Sermon on the Mount, however, cannot be restricted to the study of Matthew's Gospel for this Gospel is itself part of a larger work, the New Testament—and beyond this the entire Bible of Christians. If the whole of the Bible is affirmed as Scripture, then the Sermon on the Mount cannot be elevated to a position above the rest of the sacred text. The Reformation principle of interpreting Scripture by Scripture continues to have merit, though the way this principle is applied may differ remarkably from the methods of the Reformers.

Having stated this, however, one recognizes that the Sermon on the Mount has held a place above much of the rest of Scripture throughout the history of the church, at least in terms of aspiration if not application. This stems perhaps as much as anything from the sense many Christians have had that these three chapters more than any other part of the Bible put one in touch with the essential message and meaning of Jesus. Undoubtedly, for many the Sermon on the Mount will function as the interpretive key for *reading* the rest of the Bible, even though other passages may prove to be more determinative for how they *live out* the Bible's ethical teachings.

Matthew's Sermon on the Mount and Luke's Sermon on the Plain

The Third Gospel more nearly resembles Matthew than do Mark and John in that it includes a significant portion of the material found in the Sermon on the Mount. Mark and John have no comparable sections, although Mark does include a few of the Sermon's teachings scattered throughout the early part of his Gospel. Containing what appears to be an abbreviated version of the Sermon on the Mount, Luke has only 30 verses of teaching material in the section 6:20–49. Of these verses 21 generally correspond to material found in Matthew's 107 verses of instruction in the Sermon on the Mount. Much of what is found in the rest of Matthew's Sermon on the Mount appears in Luke in some form in other places.

An obvious difference between Matthew's Sermon on the Mount and the similar section in Luke is the setting. Matthew clearly says that when Jesus saw the crowds he *went up* on the mountain and *sat down*, accompanied by his disciples (5:1). In Luke, however, Jesus and his disciples *descended* from the mountain where they had spent the night in prayer and *stood* on a level place among a great crowd of disciples and a multitude of other people (6:17). For this reason, Luke's account is often referred to as "The Sermon on the Plain." Attempts to resolve this incongruity by reference to the topography of the supposed site of the event (i.e. a level place on the traditional "Mount of Beatitudes" above the northern shore of Lake Galilee) cannot account for all the differences in the wording of the two Gospels and fail to appreciate the different points being made by the writers.

For Luke, Jesus appears somewhat like Moses who came down from his Sinai meeting with God to speak to the Israelites camping below. Jesus descended the mountain and addressed the people who had gathered there from many places. Luke identifies three distinct groups among the people: the Twelve (whom he calls Apostles), the larger group of disciples, and a great multitude of people from such places as Judea, Jerusalem, and the seacoast area of Tyre and Sidon. Judea here probably includes Galilee and the land beyond the Jordan. Jerusalem is singled out from the rest of Judea because it deserved special mention as the center of Jewish life and because it would later be the place of Jesus' climactic activity. While Jews undoubtedly also lived in the region of Tyre and Sidon, those cities were predominately Gentile.[23] Luke apparently wanted to include Gentiles at this significant place in Jesus' ministry even though the full breakthrough in witnessing to Gentiles came later in the experience of the early church and only after much struggle (as he describes it in Acts).

Matthew's point seems to be a different one. Jesus taught *up on the mountain*. Moses did not teach on the mountaintop;

he received God's revelation there.[24] Many still hold that a primary Matthean motif concerns Jesus' Mosaic qualities: Jesus is the new Moses.[25] If a parallel exists between the mountain of the sermon and Sinai, however, it would seem to lie more in the idea that they were both places of significant revelation from God. If Matthew intends for the reader to see a connection between Jesus teaching on the mountaintop and Moses descending with God's instruction from the mountain, it may be that the stress is on Jesus as "one greater than Moses" and not on Jesus as a "new Moses."

One cannot forget, furthermore, that the final scene in the Gospel of Matthew also occurs on a mountain as Jesus sends out his disciples to teach and make disciples of all nations. The one who taught them on a mountain how to be disciples at the beginning of his ministry is also the one who from a mountain commissions them to go forth and teach others to observe all that he had commanded.

Luke's Sermon also differs from Matthew's in that the disciples to whom Jesus was speaking were not removed from the larger crowd of people. Matthew 5:1 describes Jesus sitting with his disciples up on the mountain above the crowds of people. Jesus' sermon in Luke occurs in the context of Jesus ministering to the multitude surrounding him (Luke 6:17–19). Luke does, however, indicate that the disciples were Jesus' primary audience ("He lifted up his eyes on his disciples and said . . ." 6:20), but the words were also directed toward all the people, as Luke later reveals ("After he had ended all his sayings in the hearing of the people . . ." 7:1). Matthew also indicates that the words of Jesus were heard by the crowds surrounding the open-air classroom where Jesus was instructing his disciples (Matt 7:28–29). Matthew's account gives greater weight than Luke's to the central role of the disciples, though in both Gospels the disciples and the crowds are a part of the story.

Jack Dean Kingsbury would also point to another audience for Jesus' words: the "implied reader."[26] The implied reader is a concept used in certain types of literary study to indicate the imaginary reader whom the author seems to envision as the one who can read the text with understanding and who seems to be hinted at within the text itself.[27] Kingsbury identifies the implied reader of Matthew's Gospel as a Christian living between the resurrection and Jesus' return who can look back upon Jesus' life as it is described in the Gospel and understand its significance for his or her own time. From the text one sees that the teachings for and about disciples are central not because they were directed foremost to those who followed Jesus during his earthly ministry, but because they speak to the implied reader—one who is a disciple of Jesus after his earthly ministry. The teachings of the Sermon on the Mount in Matthew describe the kind of existence such discipleship entails.

Jesus' words in the Sermon on the Mount reveal that the call to discipleship involves a radically new perspective. This call to a new perspective is dramatically expressed initially in terms of blessings. Luke's Sermon on the Plain also begins with a series of blessings. Luke, however, includes only four blessings (unlike Matthew's eight or nine) and follows these with four corresponding woes (which Matthew does not have). Matthew's wording in the first eight blessings expresses them as third person statements ("Blessed are the poor in spirit, for *theirs* is the kingdom of heaven" Matt 5:3). Luke, however, renders all four of his blessings as second person statements ("Blessed are the poor, for *yours* is the kingdom of God" Luke 6:20). Differences in precise wording also appear in each statement. Some common source probably lies behind the sermons included in both Gospels, though it is a matter of debate as to whether Matthew or Luke more nearly reflects the wording of the underlying source.

The word for "blessed" in Greek is the adjective *makarios* (here in the plural *makarioi*).[28] In the larger Greco-Roman world this term typically signified the inner happiness of those free from outward trouble, usually the gods or the rich.

In the Greek Old Testament used by most early Christians (the Septuagint) *makarios* was used of persons who were blessed by God. In wisdom writings especially, a "blessed" person was one who enjoyed the favor of God. The word did not in itself convey a blessing, but rather stated one's condition of having been blessed. The term could practically be rendered here in Matthew as "Congratulations!"

The reason for the congratulations follows the blessing ascribed to each group. The first eight beatitudes (verses 3–10) identify these groups succinctly and give an equally concise statement of the grounds for hailing each group as blessed ("Blessed are the. . . , for . . ."). The ones congratulated in each case are those exhibiting qualities indicative of kingdom life. In contrast to Matthew, Luke names only four specific groups: the poor, those presently hungry, those presently weeping, and those receiving various expressions of scorn from other people. The focus in these four beatitudes is on matters of every day existence. Poverty, hunger, and grief were the lot of Galilean peasants. The fourth beatitude, however, speaks to a condition that would have been most pronounced for Jesus' disciples—both those who had already heeded his call and those who would follow later. This fourth Lukan beatitude, which has its closest parallel in Matthew's ninth beatitude, helps to focus the other three also on those who were receptive to Jesus' teaching (particularly the disciples). The Lukan beatitudes describe the common plight of those who find themselves at odds with the power structures of the world as they encounter it. Matthew's focus has often been viewed in contrast as more "other worldly." This seems to hold at least to the degree that Jesus congratulated certain groups in this world for their experience of life already in the world yet to come.

For both Matthew and Luke, the realities of every day life are to be seen in a different light. Those who are called blessed are to see their difficult present in the light of the future. Only in this light do the very real and painful conditions of their present become signs of blessedness. Their wretchedness in the world is to be seen as a sign of their share in God's good kingdom. The coming salvation is the basis for viewing their plight in a new, positive way.

While the orientation of the Beatitudes is toward the future, they are expressed in a way which indicates that the future has already begun to impress itself upon the present. The first beatitude in Matthew (5:3) reads: "Blessed are the poor in spirit, for theirs *is* the kingdom of heaven." Luke's wording in his first beatitude differs from Matthew's in that the former reads only as "poor." In Jewish tradition the "poor" had come to represent those who stood in a relationship to God of humble dependency, in contrast to the "rich" who trusted in themselves.[29] The social reality of poverty correlated with the spiritual reality of dependency on God. Matthew's addition of the words "in spirit" highlights this religious dimension of the image of the "poor." Luke's simple reference to "poor" should not be read as though the more spiritual connotation of Matthew is absent. Yet, his Gospel does show a great sensitivity to the social reality of poverty. Those who were spiritually "poor" were also more often than not economically depressed and oppressed. Luke's beatitude speaks directly to the plight of the economically poor in a way that cannot be muted by overly "spiritualizing" his words. The vision of the kingdom given in both Gospels is one where fortunes are reversed from those which hold for the present.

The vision of God's ultimate rule found in the Beatitudes of both Gospels challenges all contemporary conditions where the rich are allowed to exploit the poor. Social, political, and ecclesiastical structures which favor the powerful and the rich are "ungodly." Disciples are not allowed the privilege of condoning, excusing, or benefiting from such structures—not even by erroneously appealing to Jesus' words about the poor always being with us as a way of exonerating ourselves from recognizing the claims another's need makes on a Christian's life. To do so puts would-be disciples on the side of those who are promised no share in the kingdom.

Matthew's second beatitude (5:4) corresponds to Luke's third (6:21b). This is more true in terms of the group congratulated than in terms of the reason for describing them as blessed. Matthew identifies them as mourners (*penthountes*); Luke calls them criers (*klaiontes*). Both terms seen in conjunction with other beatitudes hold the possibility of association with oppression.[30] Their weeping is a part of their experience of being the "have nots" in a world where the "haves" rejoice. But their suffering is not the final word; they shall be comforted. In Luke, the change from present fortunes is even more vividly evident: "Blessed are you that weep now, for you shall *laugh*."

Matthew's third beatitude (5:5) has no corresponding member among the Lukan quartet of blessings, but the fourth Matthean beatitude (5:6) matches up with Luke's second one (6:21a). While Matthew refers to "those who hunger and thirst for righteousness," Luke refers simply to those who hunger now, thereby placing greater emphasis on the problem of daily bread. Hunger was, and is, poverty's brutal friend. Hunger is no friend of God, though it may be the daily companion of God's children. Matthew's rendering, however, brings to mind that while one cannot live without bread, one does not live by bread alone. A longing of the spirit for the *right*-ness of God creates pangs of hunger in a world starving from its own self-indulgence. The kingdom vision points to change: "they shall be satisfied."

The next four beatitudes in Matthew have no counterparts in Luke. The eighth Matthean blessing (5:10), however, is somewhat similar in focus to the ninth one (5:11–12) and thus can be associated with Luke's fourth and final beatitude (6:22). Jesus' words in Matthew refer to persons being persecuted for righteousness' sake in 5:10 and to being reviled, persecuted, and having evil falsely uttered against them in 10:11. The fourth Lukan beatitude (Luke 6:22–23) cites four kinds of scorn directed toward followers of Jesus: hatred, ostracism, verbal abuse, and defamation. Verbal abuse (reviling) is the only term found in both Matthew and Luke, but the other terms are all similar in that they describe the various kinds of persecution experienced by early Christians. Disciples are to be congratulated whenever they experience such persecution for it is a sign that they are in good company—the true prophets of old who were rejected by others.

Whereas Matthew has a total of eight beatitudes (or nine if 5:11–12, which differs from the others in both form and length, counts as an additional one), Luke has only four. Luke, however, does maintain the eight-fold design of Matthew by adding four woes that correspond to the beatitudes. The four woes (Luke 6:24–26) speak of God's radical reversal of current affairs. While Matthew does not include the woes, the Beatitudes themselves point to a change in perspective that enables one to see that the status quo will not stand. The Beatitudes are good news to those who have put their trust in God and who, despite the present hardships, live in the hope-generating light of the coming kingdom.

From the point where the woes are included in the Lukan sermon, the structure begins to differ considerably from Matthew's Sermon on the Mount. Eighteen more verses throughout Matthew 5–7 find at least a rough parallel in Luke 6:27–48. Chart I below indicates which verses in Matthew parallel similar passages in Luke's Sermon on the Plain.

Interestingly, no verses from the sixth chapter of Matthew are paralleled in the sixth chapter of Luke. Twenty-two verses from Matthew 6 do appear in Luke, but they are strewn throughout the Third Gospel. In addition, other verses from chapters five and seven of Matthew are included in various places in Luke. Chart II below indicates where verses from the Sermon on the Mount are paralleled in Luke other than in the Sermon on the Plain.

Chart I Parallels between Matthew 5–7 and Luke 6:20–49

Matthew	Luke	Matthew	Luke
5:1	6:12	5:48	6:36
5:2	6:20a	7:1	6:37
5:3	6:20b	7:2b	6:38b
5:4	6:21b	7:3–5	6:41–42
5:6	6:21a	7:12	6:31
5:11–12	6:22–23	7:18	6:43
5:39	6:29	7:20	6:44
5:42	6:30	7:21	6:46
5:44	6:27	7:24–27	6:47–48
5:46	6:32–33		

Chart II Parallels between Matthew 5–7 and Rest of Luke

Matthew	Luke	Matthew	Luke
5:13–16	14:33–35	6:24	16:13
5:21–26	12:57–59	6:25–34	12:22–31
5:32	16:18	7:7–11	11:9–13
6:9–15	11:2–4	7:13–14	13:24
6:20–21	12:33–34	7:22–23	13:26–27
6:22–23	11:34–36		

The verses from the Sermon on the Mount in Chart II above have parallels in Luke in various places between 11:2 and 16:18. This section is part of a slightly larger major unit of Luke's Gospel known as the Travel Narrative (9:51–19:44).[31] This unit describes Jesus' extended journey to Jerusalem after his Galilean ministry and includes much teaching material. By describing the teaching of Jesus as something that happened "on the way" to Jerusalem, Luke may have been affirming that the life of discipleship is primarily one of pilgrimage. While this journey motif seems to reflect Luke's own theological agenda, several of the teachings that parallel parts of the Sermon on the Mount in Matthew appear in Luke in fuller contexts as far as time and place. This supports the idea that the various teachings that occur together in Matthew's Gospel may have earlier appeared separately. Such an argument does not mean that Luke's presentation is more accurate historically than Matthew's. It means, rather, that both Matthew's presentation of the teachings of Jesus in the Sermon on the Mount and Luke's presentation of Jesus' teachings in the Sermon on the Plain and elsewhere should be examined and appreciated in light of their different contexts. It also demonstrates how comparing the different presentations of the gospel story in the different Gospels can help one see what is distinctive about each Gospel.

Characteristics of the Sermon on the Mount

The above comparison of the Sermon on the Mount in Matthew with the similar section of Luke's Gospel helps to highlight the distinctiveness of the former. A closer look at the Sermon itself reveals even more of its special characteristics. Here we will examine the forms of the teachings in the Sermon, the overall design of the Sermon, and the significance of the Sermon's location within the larger Gospel of Matthew.

1. Forms of Teaching in the Sermon on the Mount

The Sermon on the Mount consists of several different types of teaching that are easily distinguishable. The Beatitudes (5:3–12) form a clear unit, as do the antitheses (5:21–48). The Lord's Prayer (6:9–13) and the closing parables (7:24–27) are also recognizable as distinct units. Much of the remainder consists of brief proverbial sayings. In fact, the short, self-contained sayings of the Sermon resemble the kind of teachings found in the Old Testament book of Proverbs. Such sayings were characteristic of the wisdom literature of the Old Testament and the Jewish wisdom tradition in general. In the New Testament the book of James provides the best parallel to the type of teaching found in the Sermon on the Mount. In fact, the teaching about swearing oaths in Matthew 5:33–37 has its only parallel in the New Testament in James 5:12. James also contains several other sayings which resemble teachings in the Sermon on the Mount and the parallel passages in Luke.

Most of the teaching in the Sermon on the Mount can be classified as "paraenesis."[32] Though the term is used in different ways by different people, it basically refers to teaching that uses general maxims, proverbs, aphorisms, and stock topics. Rather than engaging in a lengthy or complicated analysis or debate of an issue, paraenesis resorts to conventional wisdom as it is expressed in easily remembered sayings. Paraenesis is concerned to influence persons to a particular way of thinking and acting by drawing on traditions that, for the most part, are familiar to both the speaker/writer and the audience/readers. Thus, paraenesis rarely includes entirely new teachings, although the particular way traditional material is arranged and articulated may be quite different from its use elsewhere. The content of parenetic material is usually general in focus and not related to a particular situation. The selection of parenetic units and their arrangement, however, may reveal much information about the specific setting and goal of the speaker/writer.

One particular type of paraenesis found in Matthew 5–7 is the *topos*.[33] A *topos* was essentially a teaching about a specific *topic*. The teaching contained a particular ethical instruction to which were joined supporting reasons and illustrations. Matthew 6:1–4 constitutes a topic unit; the subject is piety. The initial instruction in 6:1a is explained in terms of a specific action in 6:2 (almsgiving). The motive for the action requested is given in 6b (". . . for then you will have no reward from your Father who is in heaven") and repeated in 6:4b (". . . and your Father who sees in secret will reward you"). The discussion includes rather exact clarification of the kind of behavior discouraged in 6:2a ("Thus, when you give alms, sound no trumpets before you . . .") and exemplars of those who practice the discouraged behavior in 6:2b (". . . as the hypocrites do . . ."). Others such units appear in 5:39–42; 5:44; 5:48; 6:5–8; 6:16–18; 6:19–21; 6:25–33; 6:37–38; 6:42; 7:6; 7:7–8; 7:13–14; and 7:15.

One feature of paraenesis is significantly absent from the Sermon on the Mount. Paraenesis typically uses named persons as examples, or paradigms, to support its tenets. No paradigms are included in Jesus' depiction of the life of discipleship in the Sermon on the Mount. He points to no one else as a positive example of the kind of life he is advocating. The only paradigm to be found is Jesus, himself.[34] As a parenetic summary of Jesus' perspective on discipleship, the Sermon on the Mount points to Jesus who is known by his readers as the crucified and exalted Lord. In ancient literature, such a significant sermon would probably be given as a teacher's farewell speech.[35] In Matthew, however, a sermon calling for radical righteousness based on sacrificial love comes right near the beginning of Jesus' ministry. This parenetic device has the powerful effect of connecting the ethical teachings of the Sermon on the Mount to the death and resurrection of Jesus.

2. The Design of the Sermon on the Mount

Outlines are more often imposed upon material than derived from its inherent structure. As impositions, outlines reflect the subjective concerns of the one composing them and are arbitrary. Nonetheless, some sense of structure does facilitate understanding, however inadequate the chosen design may be.

The Sermon on the Mount defies the imposition of outlines drawn too rigidly or too casually. While certain major divisions are evident in its structure, many of its parts resist being pressed into a neat pattern. Understandably then, few interpreters would devise identical outlines for their reading of the Sermon on the Mount.

A helpful approach to the design of the Sermon comes from Jack Dean Kingsbury.[36] He perceives in the Sermon a basic fivefold structure:

(1) Introduction: On Those Who Practice the Greater Righteousness (5:3–16);
(2) On Practicing the Greater Righteousness Toward the Neighbor (5:17–48);
(3) On Practicing the Greater Righteousness Before God (6:1–18);
(4) On Practicing the Greater Righteousness in Other Areas of Life (6:19–7:12);
(5) Conclusion: Injunctions on Practicing the Greater Righteousness (7:13–27).

As is apparent from this basic outline, Kingsbury finds the central thematic statement in Matthew 5:20: "For I tell you, unless your righteousness exceeds that of the scribes and Pharisees, you will never enter the kingdom of heaven."[37] The Sermon is structured around a discussion of the greater righteousness.

The introductory section can be divided into the Beatitudes (5:3–12) and the teachings on salt and light (5:13–16). Both of these sections describe what a disciple is like who does the greater righteousness. The next three major sections explain what it means to practice this greater righteousness. The second section (5:17–45) falls into two parts. The first part (5:17–20) includes statements from Jesus about his mission and his relationship to the law. The second part (5:21–48) contains six antithetical statements that stand in opposition to certain tenets of the Mosaic law.

According to Kingsbury's analysis, the central section of the Sermon is the third one (6:1–18). Formally, this section is flanked on one side by the introduction and a major section and on the other side by a major section and the conclusion. Thematically, it differs from the sections surrounding it by turning the focus to one's relationship with God and away from the issues of practicing the greater righteousness in human relationships. This third section can also be divided into three parts: (1) Alms (6:1–4); (2) Prayer (6:5–15); and (3) Fasting (6:16–18). Furthermore, the Lord's Prayer (6:9–13) stands at the center of the middle part and, thus, at the center of the entire Sermon.

The fourth section (6:19–7:12) returns to the subject of practicing the greater righteousness by treating several dimensions of life not dealt with in the second section. The section, and the Sermon, comes to a climax with the Golden Rule (7:12). The final section (7:13–27) makes the closing point that hearing the words of Jesus is inadequate; obedience is required.

The outline of the Sermon on the Mount given at the end of this Introduction is informed by Kingsbury's analysis, though it differs at those points where other divisions or terms seem more appropriate.

3. The Setting of the Sermon in Matthew

While the Sermon on the Mount stands out from the Gospel in which it appears and has legitimately commanded the attention of Christians on its own merits, most scholars would insist that due consideration be given to the literary context in which the Sermon appears. This requires careful observation of the Sermon's relationship to the rest of Matthew's Gospel.

Benjamin Bacon's study of the Sermon's place in the total structure of Matthew has influenced many.[38] He observed that Matthew can be divided into five major parts, each of which contains a narrative followed by a discourse of Jesus.

The Sermon on the Mount is the first of these major discourses and is the one which reveals the central concern of the whole Gospel. Bacon argued that this fivefold arrangement was deliberately patterned by Matthew in response to the fivefold structure of the Pentateuch of Moses (as well as other possible fivefold patterns in the Old Testament). As the new Moses, Jesus gave a new law at the outset of his ministry.

More recent study, however, has tended to reject Bacon's conclusions about the design of Matthew. For one thing, Bacon's view minimizes the significance of the Gospel's narrative by placing so much attention on the arrangement of the sermonic material. The story of the Gospel of Matthew is clearly the story of Jesus: his birth, ministry, passion, and resurrection. The focal point in this story is the passion of Jesus: his arrest, trial, crucifixion, death, and burial.

Jesus' passion was the climactic event in a series of conflicts between him and certain of the Jews. A key issue in this conflict was the relationship of the law and righteousness. Jesus' opponents understood his death to be a confirmation of the error of his views of righteousness. To their surprise (and continued disbelief), however, God raised Jesus from the grave and vindicated his ministry. His teaching about the greater righteousness prevailed through his resurrection and continued through the witness of his commissioned followers. In essence, then, this Gospel is a story about the life of Jesus and its significance.

Where does the Sermon on the Mount fit into this scheme? As already indicated above, the Sermon on the Mount points ahead to Jesus as the supreme example of discipleship. The demands of greater righteousness are fulfilled only through Jesus' sacrificial gift of himself for others. The Sermon comes early in Jesus ministry; this underscores the fact that self-giving underlies the whole of Jesus' life and teaching, and it is supposed to underlie the whole of his followers' lives. The specificity of the injunctions in the Sermon on the Mount, furthermore, stresses that disciples do practice the greater righteousness when their actions reflect the example of Jesus who gave his life for others.

How does one practice the greater righteousness of self-giving love? One way is to give up what may otherwise be considered a legitimate right to retaliation (5:38–42). Another is to refrain from passing judgement on others (7:1–5). Other specific items are given to illustrate the way disciples relate to God and the neighbor when the greater righteousness prevails. Such disciples are "blessed" and function as salt and light in the world.

The location of the Sermon on the Mount in Matthew's Gospel, then, is not accidental. The Sermon coincides with Matthew's agenda to set the superior righteousness of a suffering and saving Christ over the righteousness espoused by competing religious groups. The Sermon is the supreme place where the traditional teaching materials of Jesus are employed to instruct disciples in the way of the cross that leads to triumph.

Without doubt, the final and definitive word on the meaning and significance of the Sermon on the Mount has yet to be given. New ways of reading it constantly arise as the Sermon, along with the rest of Scripture, persistently challenges a changing world. The enduring, and yet equally confounding, challenge of the Sermon on the Mount is its unrelenting summons to a higher way. The word from the mountain stands above us and calls us upward.

An Outline of
THE SERMON ON THE MOUNT

Notes

[1]W. S. Kissinger, *The Sermon on the Mount: A History of Interpretation and Bibliography.* ATLA Bibliography Series 3 (Meteuchen, NJ: Scarecrow Press, 1975) 6.

[2]*Summa Theologica* I, IIae. cvii–cviii. Trans. the Fathers of the English Dominican Province. (New York: Benziger Bros., inc., 1947).

[3]*Luther's Works*, Vol. 21: *The Sermon on the Mount and the Magnificat,* ed. Jeroslav Pelikan (St. Louis: Concordia Publishing House, 1956) 113.

[4]*Commentary on the Harmony of the Evangelists, Matthew, Mark, and Luke*, Vol. 1 (Grand Rapids: Eerdmans, 1949).

[5]Eduard Thurneysen, *The Sermon on the Mount*, trans. William C. Robinson (Richmond: John Knox Press, 1963).

[6]See the discussions of the Anabaptists and others in Robert A. Guelich, "Interpreting the Sermon on the Mount," *Interpretation* 41 (1987):119 and Georg Strecker, *The Sermon on the Mount: An Exegetical Commentary*, trans. O. C. Dean, Jr. (Nashville: Abingdon Press, 1988) 16–17.

[7]A thorough discussion of Tolstoy's approach is given by Clarence Bauman, *The Sermon on the Mount: The Modern Quest for Its Meaning* (Macon: Mercer University Press, 1985) 11–35.

[8]See Guelich, "Interpreting the Sermon on the Mount," 121 and Bauman 37–51.

[9]Rudolf Bultmann, *Jesus and the Word*, trans. Louise P. Smith and Erminie H. Lantero (London: Collins, 1958). See the discussions of Bultmann's views by Strecker, 21 and Bauman, 197–207.

[10]Rudolf Bultmann, *History of the Synoptic Tradition*, trans. John Marsh, rev. ed. (New York: Harper& Row, 1963) 65–68.

[11]Günther Bornkamm, *Jesus of Nazareth*, trans. Irene and Fraser McLuskey with James M. Robinson (New York: Harper & Row, 1960) 87.

[12]A complete discussion of the history of religion school is given by Werner Georg Kümmel, *The New Testament: The History of the Investigation of Its Problems*, trans. S. MacLean and Howard Clark Kee (Nashville: Abingdon, 1972).

[13]Johannes Weiss, *Jesus' Proclamation of the Kingdom*, trans. Richard H. Hiers and David L. Holland (Philadelphia: Fortress, 1971).

[14]Schweitzer's famous position about the Sermon on the Mount as an "interim ethic" appears prominently in two of his works: *The Quest of the Historical Jesus. A Critical Study of Its Progress from Reimarus to Wrede*, trans. W. Montgomery (London: Adam & Charles Black, 1910) and *The Kingdom of God and Primitive Christianity*, trans. L. A. Garrard (London: Adam & Charles Black, 1968). See also Bauman's discussion, 111–127.

[15]*The New Scofield Reference Bible* (Oxford: Oxford University Press, 1967).

[16]As Bauman shows (75–93), Naumann's views changed radically through the several stages of his career. His final dismissal of the relevance of the ethics of the Sermon on the Mount appear in his *Briefe über Religion (mit Nachwort nach 13 Jahren)* (Berlin: Druck und Verlag von Georg Reimer, 1916). See also Strecker, 17–18.

[17]Hans Windisch, *The Meaning of the Sermon on the Mount: A Contribution to the Historical Understanding of the Gospels and to the Problem of Their True Exegesis*, trans. S. MacLean Gilmour (Philadelphia: Westminster Press, 1951).

[18]Hermann Strack and Paul Billerbeck, *Kommentar zum Neuen Testament aus Talmud und Midrasch*, 6 vols. (Munich: Beck, 1922–1961) and Gerhard Kittel, "Die Bergpredigt und die Ethik des Judentums," *Zeitschrift für systematische Theologie* 2 (1925): 555–94.

[19]W. D. Davies, *The Setting of the Sermon on the Mount* (Cambridge: Cambridge University Press, 1964).

[20]Georg Strecker, *The Sermon on the Mount: An Exegetical Commentary*, trans. O. C. Dean, Jr. (Nashville: Abingdon, 1988).

[21]Hans Dieter Betz, *Essays on the Sermon on the Mount* (Philadelphia: Fortress Press, 1985).

[22]John P. Meier, *Law and History in Matthew's Gospel: A Redactional Study of Mt. 5:17–48,* Analecta biblica 71 (Rome: Biblical Institute Press, 1976) and Robert A. Guelich, *The Sermon on the Mount: A Foundation for Understanding* (Waco: Word Publishers, 1982).

[23]Fred B.Craddock, *Luke,* Interpretation: A Bible Commentary for Teaching and Preaching (Louisville: John Knox Press, 1990) 86.

[24]Frank Stagg, "Matthew," *The Broadman Bible Commentary,* vol. 8 (Nashville: Broadman Press, 1969) 104.

[25]Davies 107.

[26]Jack Dean Kingsbury, "The Place, Structure, and Meaning of the Sermon on the Mount," *Interpretation* 61 (1987): 135.

[27]For a clear, concise discussion of the concept of the "implied reader," see Mark Allan Powell, *What Is Narrative Criticism?,* Guides to Biblical Scholarship (Philadelphia: Fortress Press, 1990) 19–21.

[28]I. Howard Marshall, *Commentary on Luke,* New International Greek Testament Commentary (Grand Rapids: Eerdmans, 1978) 245–249.

[29]Charles H. Talbert, *Reading Luke: a Literary and Theological Commentary on the Third Gospel* (New York: Crossroad, 1982) 71.

[30]Marshall 250–51.

[31]Warren McWilliams, "Travel Narrative," *Mercer Dictionary of the Bible* (Macon: Mercer University Press, 1990) 929–30.

[32]Discussions of the nature of paraenesis are given in James G. Williams, "Paraenesis, Excess, and Ethics: Matthew's Rhetoric in the Sermon on the Mount," *Semeia* 50 (1990): 163–4 and Abraham J. Malherbe *Moral Exhortation, A Greco-Roman Sourcebook,* Library of Early Christianity (Philadelphia: Westminster Press, 1986) 124–5.

[33]Williams 170–1.

[34]Ibid 170.

[35]Ibid 181.

[36]Kingsbury, "The Place, Structure, and Meaning of the Sermon on the Mount" 136–42.

[37]Ibid 136. This point is also made by W. Clyde Tilley, *The Surpassing Righteousness: Evangelism and Ethics in the Sermon on the Mount* (Greenville: Smyth & Helwys, 1992).

[38]Benjamin Bacon, *Studies in Matthew* (London: Constable, 1930).

Recommended for Further Study

Augsburger, Myron S. *The Expanded Life: The Sermon on the Mount for Today.* New York: Abingdon, 1972.

Alt, Franz, *Peace Is Possible: The Politics of the Sermon on the Mount.* New York: Schocken Books, 1985.

Bacon, Benjamin W. "Jesus and the Law: A Study for the First 'Book' of Matthew (Mt. 3–7)."*Journal of Biblical Literature* 47 (1928): 207–08.

_____. *Studies in Matthew.* London: Constable, 1930.

Barnette, Henlee H. "The Ethic of the Sermon on the Mount."*Review and Expositor* 53 (1956): 23–33.

Batdorf, I. W. "How Shall We Interpret the Sermon on the Mount?"*Journal of Bible and Religion* 27 (3, 1959): 211–17.

Bauman, Clarence. *The Sermon on the Mount: The Modern Quest for Its Meaning.* Macon, GA: Mercer University Press, 1985.

Betz, Hans Dieter. *Essays on the Sermon on the Mount.* Philadelphia: Fortress, 1985.

_____. "The Hermeneutical Principles of the Sermon on the Mount."*Journal of Theology for South Africa* 42 (1983): 17–28.

_____. "The Sermon on the Mount: Its Literary Genre and Function."*Journal of Religion* 59 (1979): 285–297.

Bligh, J. *The Sermon on the Mount. A Discussion on Mt 5–7.* Slough, 1975.

Boice, James. *The Sermon on the Mount.* Grand Rapids: Eerdmans, 1972.

Bonhoeffer, Dietrich. *The Cost of Discipleship.* Translated by R. H. Fuller. New York: Macmillan Publishing Co. 1963.

Burchard, C. "The Theme of the Sermon on the Mount,"in *Essays on the*

Love Commandment. Edited by R. H. Fuller. Philadelphia: Fortress, 1978.

Carlston, Charles E. "Recent American Interpretations of the Sermon on the Mount."*Bangalore Theological Forum* 17 (1985): 9–22.

Carson, D. A. *The Sermon on the Mount. An Evangelical Exposition of Matthew 5–7.* Grand Rapids: Baker Book House, 1978.

Catchpole, David, "The Sermon on the Mount in Today's World." *Theology and Evangelism* 14 (1981) 4–11.

Davies, W. D. *The Sermon on the Mount.* Cambridge: Cambridge University Press, 1966.

_____. *The Setting of the Sermon on the Mount.* Cambridge: Cambridge University Press, 1964.

Dibelius, Martin. *The Sermon on the Mount.* New York: Charles Scribner's Sons, 1940.

Drumwright, H. L., "The Ethical Motif in Mt 5–7."*Southwestern Journal of Theology* 5 (1962): 65–76.

Ellis, P. F., "Matthew: His Mind and His Message. The Sermon on the Mount—the Authority of Jesus 'in Word' Mt 5:1–7:29."*Bible Today* 70 (1974): 1483–91.

Fisher, Fred L. *The Sermon on the Mount.* Nashville: Broadman Press, 1976.

Friedlander, Gerald. *The Jewish Sources of the Sermon on the Mount.* London: Routledge & Kegan Paul, 1910.

Gibbs, J. M., "The Son of God as the Torah Incarnate in Matthew,"*Studia Evangelica*, IV (1968): 38–46.

Gilmour, S. MacLean. "Interpreting the Sermon on the Mount."*Crozer Quarterly* 24 (1947): 47–56.

Gore, Charles. *The Sermon on the Mount: A Practical Exposition.* London: John Murray, 1900.

Grant, R. M. "The Sermon on the Mount in Early Christianity."*Semeia* 12 (1978): 215–31.

Greenwood, D. "Moral Obligation in the Sermon on the Mount." *Theological Studies* 31 (1970): 301–309.

Guelich, Robert A. *The Sermon on the Mount. A Foundation for Understanding.* Waco, TX: Word Books, 1982.

HaRing, B. "The Normative Value of the Sermon on the Mount."*Catholic Biblical Quarterly* 29 (1967): 375–85.

Hendrickx, Hermann. *The Sermon on the Mount.* London: Geoffrey Chapman, 1984.

Hickling, C. J. A. "Conflicting Motives in the Redaction of Matthew: Some Condsiderations on the Sermon on the Mount and Matthew 18:15–20,"in *StudEv.* VII (1982,) 247–260.

Hill, David. "The Meaning on the Sermon on the Mount in Matthew's Gospel." *Irish Biblical Studies* 6 (1984): 120–133.

Hunter, Archibald Macbride. *Design for Life; An Exposition of the Sermon on the Mount, Its Making, Its Exegisis, and Its Meaning.* London: SCM Press, 1965.

_____. "The Meaning of the Sermon on the Mount."*Expository Times* LXIII (1952): 176–79.

Jeremias, Joachim. *The Sermon on the Mount.* Translated by Norman Perrin. Philadelphia: Fortress Press, 1963.

Jordan, Clarence. *Sermon on the Mount.* Valley Forge, PA: Judson Press, 1952.

Keck, L. E. "The Sermon on the Mount." In *Jesus and Man's Hope,* Donald G. Miller and Dikran Y. Hadidian, eds. Pittsburgh: Pittsburgh Theological Seminary, 1971.

Kingsbury, Jack. *Matthew: Structure, Christology, Kingdom.* Philadelphia: Fortress, 1975.

_____. *Matthew as Story*. Philadelphia, 1986.

Kissinger, Warren S. *The Sermon on the Mount: A History of Interpretation and Bibliography*. ATLA Bibliography Series, Number 3. Metuchen, N.J.: Scarecrow Press, 1975.

Krause, C. "The Sermon on the Mount in Ecumenical Thought Since World War II."*Lutherische Rundschau* 18 (1968): 65–74.

Lachs, S. T., "Some Textual Observations on the Sermon on the Mount."*Jewish Quarterly Review* 69 (1978): 98–111.

Lambrecht, Jan. *The Sermon on the Mount: Proclamation and Exhortation*, Good News Studies 14 (Wilmington, DE: Michael Glazier, 1985).

Lapide, P. E. *The Sermon on the Mount: Utopia or Program for Action?* Mary Knoll, N.Y.: Orbis, 1986.

Lloyd-Jones, Martin, *Studies in the Sermon on the Mount*, 2 Volumes. Grand Rapids: Eerdmans, 1959–1960.

LuThi, W. & Brunner, R. *The Sermon on the Mount*. 1963.

Marriott, Horace. *The Sermon on the Mount*. New York/Toronto: Macmillan, 1925.

McArthur, Harvey K. *Understanding the Sermon on the Mount*. London: The Epworth Press, 1961.

McEleney, N. J. "The Principles of the Sermon on the Mount." *Catholic Biblical Quarterly* 41 (1979): 552–70.

Neirynck, F. "The Sermon on the Mount in the Gospel Synopsis." *Evangelica* 60 (1982): 729–36.

Ohrn, Arnold T. *The Gospel and The Sermon on the Mount*. New York: Fleming H. Revell Co., 1984.

Pentecost, J. Dwight. *The Sermon on the Mount*. Contemporary Insights for a Christian Lifestyle. Portland OR: Multnomah Press, 1980.

Pentecost, J. Dwight. "The Purpose of the Sermon on the Mount."*Bibliotheca Sacra* 115 (1958): 313–19.

Roberts, J. H. "The Sermon on the Mount and the Idea of Liberty." *Neotestamentica* 1 (1967): 9–15.

Schnackenburg, Rudolf. "The Sermon on the Mount and Modern Man." In *Christian Existence in the New Testament* , I. Notre Dame, 1968.

Shinn, Roger L. *The Sermon on the Mount.* Philadelphia: United Church Press, 1962.

Skibbe, E. M. "Pentateuchal Themes in the Sermon on the Mount." *Lutheran Quarterly* 20 (1968): 44–51.

Thielicke, Helmut. *Life Can Begin Again. Sermons on the Sermon on the Mount.* 1963.

Thurneysen, Eduard. *The Sermon on the Mount.* Translated by W. C. Robinson and J. M. Robinson. Richmond VA: John Knox Press, 1964.

Tuttle, G.A. "The Sermon on the Mount: Its Wisdom Affinities and Their Relation to Its Structure."*Journal of the Evangelical Theology Society* 20 (1977): 213–30.

Waylen, Hector. *Mountain Pathways: A Study in the Ethics of the Sermon on the Mount.* London: Sherratt & Hughes, 1909.

Williams, James G. "Paraenesis, Ethics, and Excuses: Matthew's Rhetoric in the Sermon on the Mount."*Semeia* 50 (1990): 163-187.

Windisch, Hans. *The Meaning of the Sermon on the Mount: A Contribution to the Historical Understanding of the Gospels and to the Problem of Their True Exegisis.* Translated by S. MacLean Gilmour. Philadelphia: The Westminster Press, 1951.

Wood, James. *The Sermon on the Mount and its Application.* London: Geoffrey Bles, 1963.

Chapter One

The Cotton Patch Version of the Sermon on the Mount

Matthew 5–7

by Clarence Jordan

1. When Jesus saw the larger crowd, he went up the hill and sat down. His students gathered around him, and he began teaching them, and this is what he said:

"The spiritually humble are God's people, for they are citizens of His new Order.

They who are deeply concerned are God's people, for they will see their ideas become reality.

They who are gentle are His people, for they will be His partners across the land.

They who have an unsatisfied appetite for the right are God's people, for they will be given plenty to chew on.

The generous are God's people, for they will be treated generously.

They whose motives are pure are God's people, for they will have spiritual insight.

Men of peace and good will are God's people, for they will be known throughout the land as His children.

They who have endured much for what's right are God's people; they are citizens of His new Order.

You all are God's people when others call you names, and harass you and tell all kinds of false tales on you just because you follow me. Be cheerful and good-humored, because your spiritual advantage is great. For that's the way they treated men of conscience in the past.

13. You are all the earth's salt. But now if *you* just sit there and don't salt, how will the world ever get salted? You'll be so worthless that you will be thrown out and trampled on by the rest of society. You are the world's light; you are a city on a hill that cannot be hid. Have you ever heard of anybody turning on a light and then covering it up? Don't you fix it so that it will light up the whole room? Well, then, since you are God's light which he has turned on, go ahead and shine so clearly that when your conduct is observed it will plainly be the work of your spiritual Father.

17. Don't ever think that I'm trying to destroy the moral and religious principles of our way of life. My purpose is not to destroy them but to establish them. For I truthfully tell you that so long as heaven and earth remain, not one dotting of an 'i' or crossing of a 't' will be eliminated from our highest and noblest ideals until every one of them becomes a reality. So then, if anyone disregards one of the least of these God-given principles, and encourages others to do so, he shall be considered unimportant in the New Order of the Spirit. But whoever lives by them and upholds them shall be considered vital to the new Order of the Spirit.

20. And let me tell you something else: Unless *your* conduct is better than that of the usual. ordinary religious people, you will never make the grade into God's New Order of the Spirit. For example, you have always been told, 'Don't murder,' and 'if anyone does murder, he shall be brought to judgement.' But I'm telling you that everyone who nurses a grudge against his fellow man shall be brought into judge-

ment. And anyone who spits in the face of his brother stands condemned, and whoever yells, 'You low-down so-and-so,' shall be roasted in hell's fires. So then, if you are in worship services and keep remembering all the things your brother has against you, leave the sanctuary and go look up the one you have wronged and straighten things out with him. Only then may you return to church.

25. Be courteous at all times toward an opponent. Otherwise, you might be dragged into court, turned over to the sheriff and thrown into the clink. I'm telling you a fact, you won't get out of there until you have paid the last cent of your fine.

27. You've heard it said, 'Don't sleep with someone you're not married to.' But I want to warn you, whoever sets his eye on a woman with the hope of intercourse with her has already slept with her in his mind. So if your right eye becomes hopelessly infected, have it cut out and thrown away, because it is better to lose one of your organs than to lose your whole body. Or if your right hand becomes hopelessly infected, cut it off and throw it away, because it is better to lose one of your limbs than to lose your whole body.[1]

31. It has also been said, 'If a man divorces his wife, let him give her a certificate that she is free.' But I'm telling you all, anyone who divorces his wife except for sleeping with another man causes her to have had an unlawful intercourse, and whoever marries one so divorced also has had unlawful intercourse.

33. Again you have heard it said by the old folks, 'Don't break your oath, and always keep a solemn oath to the Lord.' But I'm telling you not to make any oaths at all—not by the heaven, as God's throne; or by the earth, as his foot-rest; or

by Jerusalem, as 'the city of the Great King.' Don't make an oath even by your head, because you can't make one hair black or white. Instead, let your word be a straight-forward *yes* or *no*. If it takes more than that, it's bad.

38. You've also heard the saying, 'Take an eye for an eye; take a tooth for a tooth.' But I'm telling you, *never* respond with evil. Instead, if somebody slaps you on your right cheek, offer him the other one too. And if anybody wants to drag you into court and take away your shirt, let him have your undershirt. If somebody makes you go a mile for him, go two miles. Give to him who asks of you, and don't turn your back on anyone who wants a loan.

43. Another thing you've always heard is, 'Love your own group and hate the hostile outsider.' But I'm telling you, love the outsiders and pray for those who try to do you in, so that you might be sons of your spiritual Father. For he lets his sun rise on both sinners and saints, and he sends rain on both good people and bad. Listen here, if you love only those who love you, what is your advantage? Don't even scalawags do that much? And if you speak to no one but your friends, how are you any different? Do not the non-Christians do as much? Now you, you all must be mature, as your spiritual father is mature.

6

1. See to it that your effort to do right is not based on a desire to be popular. If it is, you'll get no help from your spiritual Father. For instance, when you make a gift to charity, don't make a lot of noise about it, like the phonies do at church and at civic clubs, so as to be praised by their cronies. The truth is, such praise is all they'll get out of it. But you, when you give to charity, don't pat yourself on the back, so that your gift might be truly secret. And your Father, who sees secrets, will respond to you.

5. And when you pray, don't be like the phonies. For they love to stand up and pray in church and at public occasions, so they might build a reputation as pray-ers. The truth is, that's all they'll get out of it. But you, when you pray, go to your bedroom, shut the door and pray to your Father in private. And your seeing Father will privately participate with you. And while you are praying, don't jabber like pagans, who think that their long-windedness will get them an answer. Don't you be like them, for your Father knows what you need before you ever ask him. So here's the way you all should pray:

> 'Father of us, O Spiritual One,
> Your name be truly honored.
> Your kingdom spread, your will prevail
> Through earth, as through the heavens.
> Sustaining bread grant us each day.
> Forgive our debts as we forgive
> The debts of all who cannot pay.
> And from confusion keep us clear;
> Deliver us from evil's sway.'

For if you forgive men when they wrong you, your spiritual Father will forgive you, too. But if you don't forgive others, neither will your Father forgive your wrongs.

16. Now when you go to church, don't be like the religious phonies who put on a solemn face to impress men with their piety. Rather, when you go to church, act perfectly normal so as not to give the impression you're going there to be seen, but to worship God. And your Father, who discerns the inner motive, will participate with you.

19. Put no value on earthly possessions, which worms and rust consume, and which thieves break into and steal. Rather, you all set your hearts on spiritual values, which neither

worms nor rust consume, and which thieves do not break into and steal. For your values and your character are wrapped up together.

22. The body depends on the eyes for light. Now if your eyes are in focus, then the body will have clear light. But if your eyes are not in focus,[2] then your whole body will be in confused darkness. Now if your life is so divided, you're *really* in the dark! That's why it is impossible for a man to serve *two* masters. For he will hate one of them and love the other; he will have respect for one and contempt for the other! It is *impossible* to be in bondage to both God and money.

25. Therefore, let me tell you all something: Don't worry about making a living—what you'll eat, what you'll drink, what you'll wear. Isn't the life of a man more important than what he eats? And isn't the health of the body more important than clothing? Think for a moment about the birds of the sky. They don't plant. They don't harvest. they don't store up in barns. Even so, your spiritual Father cares for them. Really now, aren't you all more precious than *birds*? Besides, who of you, by fretting and fuming, can make himself one inch taller?

28. And what's all this big to-do over clothing? Look yonder at that field of flowers, how they are growing. They do no house-work and no sewing. But I'm telling you, not even Solomon in all his finery was ever dressed up like one of them. Well then, if God so clothes the flowers of the field which are blooming today and are used for fuel tomorrow, won't he do even more for you, you spiritual runts? So cut out your anxious talk about 'what are we gonna eat, and what are we gonna drink, and what are we gonna wear.' For the people of the world go tearing around after all *these* things. Listen, your spiritual Father is quite aware that

you've got to have all such stuff. Then set your heart on the God Movement and its kind of life, and all these things will come as a matter of course. Don't worry over the future; let the future worry over itself. Each day has enough trouble of its own.

7

1. Don't preach just to keep from being preached to. For the same sermon you preach will be applied to you, and the stuff you dish out to others will be dished up to you. Why examine the splinter in your brother's eye, and take no notice of the plank in your own eye? Or how can you say to your brother, 'Bud, hold still while I pick that splinter out of your eye,' when there is a plank in yours? Listen, you phoney, first pull the plank from your eye and then you'll be able to see better to get the splinter out of your brother's eye.

6. 'Don't throw your valuables to the dogs,
   And don't spread your pearls before the hogs;
   Or they will trample them under their feet
   And even turn and bite you.'

7. Start asking and it will be given to you; start looking and you will find; start knocking, and the door will be opened to you. For every asker receives, and every seeker finds, and to every one who knocks the door shall be opened. For is there any man among you whose son shall ask him for bread and he'll give him a rock? Or if he should ask for a fish, will he give him a snake? Well then, if you, weak mortals that you are, are capable of making good gifts to your children, don't you think your spiritual Father will give even better gifts to those who ask him?

12. Therefore, in all your dealings with people, treat them as you want to be treated. This, in a nutshell, is the essence of all our moral and religious principles.

13. Approach life through the gate of discipline. For the way that leads to emptiness is wide and easy, and a lot of folks are taking that approach. But the gate into the full life is hard, and the road is bumpy, and only a few take this route.

15. Keep your eye peeled for fake preachers, who come to you with sheepskins from wolf-schools. You'll be able to distinguish them by the way they live. You know, you don't gather grapes from a bramble bush nor peaches from a chinaberry, do you? So it is, a cultivated tree makes cultivated fruit, and a wild tree makes wild fruit. It is impossible for a cultivated tree to bear wild fruit, or for a wild tree to bear cultivated fruit. Any tree that does not produce cultivated fruit is chopped down and thrown into the fire. That's why I told you that you could know them by the way they *live*.

21. Not everyone who glibly calls me 'Lord, Lord,' shall enter the Order of the Spirit, but he who *does* the will of my Spiritual Father. The time will come when many people will gather around and say, 'L-o-ord, oh L-o-o-rd, *we* sure did preach in your name, didn't we? And in your name *we* sure did give the devil a run for his money, didn't we? *We* did all kinds of stunts in your name, didn't we? Then I'll admit right in front of everybody that I've never known you. Get away from me you wicked religious racketeers.

24. That's why the man who hears these words of mine and acts on them shall be like a wise man who built his house on the rock. Down came the rain, up rose the floods, out lashed the winds. They all beset that house, but it did not fall. It was on *rock* foundation.

26. And the man who hears these words of mine and fails to act on them shall be like an idiot who built his house on the sand. Down came the rain, up rose the floods, out lashed

the winds. They all cut at that house, and it fell! And my, what a collapse!"

28. When Jesus finished speaking, the people were simply amazed at his teaching, for he was teaching them like he knew what he was talking about. He didn't sound like *their* preachers.

Notes

[1] The argument here seems to be that sex, a God-given function like the eye or the hand, may become the focal point of moral infection and cause the destruction of the whole personality. Under these conditions, like a badly infected eye or hand, it is better to give up sex than to let it ruin one's whole life.

[2] That is, with one eye on one thing, the other on something else.

Chapter Two

When Down Is Up

Matthew 5:1–3

by David W. Crocker

It is true, isn't it? Things are not always as they appear to be. Pat Neff, one time governor of Texas and later President of Baylor University, told of two school teachers who met back on campus after having not seen each other for many years. Their conversation went something like this:

The first lady said to her friend, "I've gotten married since we last met."

The second replied, "Oh, that's good."

The first responded, "Well, I don't know about that. My husband is twice as old as I am."

The second replied, "Oh, that's bad."

The first answered, "Well, I don't know about that. He's worth a million dollars."

The second said, "Oh, that's good."

The first said, "Well, I don't know about that. He won't give me a cent."

The second responded, "Oh, that's bad."

The first said, "Well, I don't know about that. He did build me a $200,000 house."

The second said, "Oh, that's good."

The first replied, "Well, I don't know about that. It burned down last week."

The second responded, "Oh, that's bad."
The first said, "Well, I don't know about that . . . ; he was in it."[1]

Things are not always as they appear to be. Good appears as bad; bad appears as good. Opportunity comes knocking as crisis; suffering lurks in the shadows of prosperity. On and on it goes. Things are *not* always as they appear.

This is one of the keys to understanding the Beatitudes. Standing on the hillside just up from the beautiful Sea of Galilee, gazing over the swarm of people who had gathered to see what he might do next, Jesus took society's standards of happiness and turned them upside down. He saw them trying to "make it" by those materialistic, self-centered criteria and said, "Stop! You've got it all wrong! What you thought was down is up. What you have seen as empty is really full. What you thought was lowly is actually the beginning of exaltation. So stop knocking yourselves out for dreams that cannot satisfy. See God's way to contentment and happiness, and give up to it!"

Here we are nearly two thousand years later and we still haven't understood him or believed him. We are just as locked into the old criteria for happiness—property, popularity, and power—the three "P's" of happiness as the masses who sat at his feet when he first gave the Beatitudes. We still haven't recognized that Jesus replaced them with his own criteria—humility, meekness, mercy, peace, and so on.

No wonder we're still not happy. We're going about it all wrong. We're looking in the wrong places—in the Dow Jones Report or in a list of our personal assets; in the ivy halls of education or in the achievements of our children. We're listening to the wrong people—Jesse Jackson, Ronald Reagan, Phil Donahue, Bill Cosby, Richard Simmons, Dr. Ruth, when we ought to be listening to Jesus. In these sermons on the Beatitudes we will listen to Jesus again as he gives his criteria for contentment. I encourage you to open yourselves to this new way of looking at happiness.

I

Matthew says Jesus saw the crowds of people who had gathered, and he says it in such a way as to lead us to believe that the very sight of the masses moved Jesus to find a place suitable for teaching that he might give them something to live by. When Jesus looked at people, he saw more than we usually see. Not that he had some kind of special x-ray vision which enabled him to know the deepest, darkest secrets of those around him, but that he looked with a unique understanding and feeling for people. I think Clarence Jordan has it right when he says:

> Crowds always moved Jesus. Sometimes the sight of them moved him to great compassion; at other times their disbelief aroused his pity; their selfishness caused him to wonder if they were following him only for the loaves and fishes; . . . and their lostness and confusion filled him with a desire to show them the true way to life.[2]

So he sat down to speak to them, and they were all ears. "Happy are the poor in spirit, for the kingdom of heaven belongs to them," he said. But what did he mean? On the surface of it, the first part of the first Beatitude appears to be a contradiction in terms—the poor in spirit are happy. Indeed, not having much spirit and happiness do appear to be mutually exclusive in their meaning. But, remember, things are not always as they appear.

In order to understand what Jesus meant in the first Beatitude, we will have to do a little word study. The word translated "poor" does not mean merely not having much or being without money or property. It is the word used to refer to extreme poverty. It means completely destitute, to lead the life of a beggar. In ancient Greek Homer used this word to describe a suppliant beggar. Herodotus used it to describe a person who had been rich and well to do but is now reduced to begging for scraps from the table.[3] If we were writing in Greek today, we would use this word to refer to the pitiful homeless who roam from one place to another living from one handout to another.

Look how Jesus used this word. He used it to describe the character Lazarus in the parable of Dives and Lazarus (Luke 16:19-31). Lazarus was the poor man who sat outside Dives' gate and begged for the leftover from Dives' sumptuous table. Jesus used this word to describe the widow who gave her last two pennies as a vivid illustration of sacrificial giving (Mark 12:41-44). This word "poor" is not just substandard; it is pathetically poor, wretchedly poor.

And when it is combined with the phrase "in spirit" —"poor in spirit," it takes on another meaning. To be poor in spirit is to be utterly humble. It is to acknowledge one's own helplessness, to recognize one's own circumstance of being without reason for pride.

It is important that we understand that Jesus was not speaking of those people who do not have much materially or financially when he gave the first Beatitude. As one preacher put it:

> The gospel does not elevate a mere lack of money. The poor are not to be revered because they are poor. Christ chose to leave heaven not because he despised the riches of glory or adored the poverty of earth. His earthly poverty didn't make him Savior and Lord. His willingness to submit himself to the Father did.[4]

And that's just what he meant when he said, "Happy are the poor in spirit. . . ."

You want a picture? Jesus gave plenty of them. There once were two men in church. Both of them were praying. One of them stood and prayed loud enough for all present to hear. One by one he named his spiritual victories—not giving in to temptation, strict obedience of the church's rules, and so on. Oh, he was a paragon of virtue, this saint.

The other man did not stand when he prayed. In fact he went into a corner by himself and knelt down on the stone floor of the sanctuary. Hardly anyone could hear him. That was because he whispered and wept as he prayed as if he was ashamed to talk to God. All he said was "I'm sorry, please forgive me. I'm sorry for this sin. I'm sorry for that sin. Be merciful to me, Lord." That's "poor in spirit" in living color.

II

Now I ask you: Is there anything more difficult for us to accept than that? I say accept because we really don't have much trouble understanding, do we? It's believing we have trouble with, translating our understanding into conviction.

Let's be honest. We who live in an achievement-oriented, success-dominated society do not want to hear Jesus say that the real way to happiness is by being poor in spirit. We have managed to maintain the tricky position of being Christians while holding onto popular standards of success. We have even revised theology to support our commitment to success and encouraged the prophets of prosperity who are only too willing to tell us what we want to hear—that God wants you to be happy . . . and prosperous . . . and successful . . . and popular. And he will help you get it.

Recently, in a seminar held in our church, Beverly Terrell of Houston, Texas, told an extraordinary story which illustrates our trouble with the first Beatitude. Years ago, when Beverly's boys were still young and she was at the peak of her singing career, something happened. She was in great demand as a concert artist, booked up two years in advance. Then, as she was preparing for her first major concert with a symphony orchestra, her singing voice left her. She could speak but she could not sing. This was the first time this had ever happened to her.

Beverly Terrell is not only a fine singer, she is also an ardent student and teacher of singing. She understands how proper sounds are made with the human voice and how to avoid the common problems often associated with a career in singing. She teaches all her students about the improper ways of singing which bring on laryngitis. She knew all this, but she was suddenly stricken with laryngitis herself.

She went to one of the finest laryngologists, or "throat doctors," she could find. He did all the tests he knew to do but he could not find her problem. He was baffled. Here was a woman who was an accomplished singer, schooled in the proper singing techniques, and thoroughly acquainted with the pitfalls of poor singing that cause problems. She could speak, but she could not sing.

Not knowing what else to do, the doctor referred Beverly to a psychiatrist. Beverly said she had never been so angry. She said, "You doctors! If you can't diagnose a problem, either you call it a virus or you assume it's psychosomatic." And she proceeded to tell the doctor what he could do with his referral.

She didn't go to the psychiatrist, but neither did she get her voice back for some time. She fretted and fussed. "If I don't get my voice back," she said, "I'll die. I can't go through life not being able to sing."

Then one day while she was acting out her frustration by furiously cleaning her house and crying and praying, it suddenly dawned on her what had happened. It was when she asked God why this had happened to her that he revealed to her how pride dominated her life. She says that she had become the center of her own life. Everything she did was done to impress people—the music she chose to sing, the kinds and places of concerts, the way she would stand around when she'd finished singing to receive lavish compliments, the way she dressed, the kind of car she drove—everything was designed to impress others. It was a truly confronting, shaming experience, and Beverly did not try to argue against it. She said, "Oh, God, I'm so sorry." For two hours she stayed on her knees in her bedroom crying and confessing to God. He would show her another sin and she would confess it. And all the while the vacuum cleaner was running.

That's being poor in spirit—contrite and destitute before a gracious and forgiving God. Beverly Terrell's experience shows why we who are achievement-oriented have such trouble with it.[5]

III

But there is more to this Beatitude. All of them finish with a promise. They begin with a statement of condition for contentment and they finish with the source of that contentment. In this first Beatitude the promise is nothing less than the kingdom of heaven: "Happy are the poor in spirit, for the kingdom of heaven belongs to them."

Do you know what the kingdom of heaven is? It's not heaven itself, at least not as we normally think of it—the eternal afterlife which all of us who are believers eagerly await. The kingdom of heaven (or the kingdom of God as it is sometimes said) is the rule of God in one's life. It's when God is given absolute authority in life, when his word is final in every matter, and when his will is the priority in all behavior. William Barclay has said it this way: "To be a citizen of the kingdom of God . . . [or] to possess the kingdom of God . . . means perfectly to accept the will of God."[6] To put it another way, to have the kingdom of heaven is to be in perfect tune with his will.

Now that's happiness! No more alienation from the source of life. No more loneliness from the holy presence we require for fullness. No more emptiness from the unconditional love we were created to receive. That's contentment, beautiful, peaceful, abiding contentment. It does not come as the result of an all-out search or strict discipline or an inheritance, but as a discovery of the end of the road called humility.

Ever since James Hilton wrote his book, *Lost Horizon*, the name "Shangri-La" has been synonymous with happiness. But you might be surprised to know that the place reported to be the fabled, ever-happy, heaven-on-earth Shangri-La is not what it's cracked up to be. A camera technician who went to that spot in the Himalayas with a film company was shocked by what he found there—a valley of barren rocks and scrub growth and lean children dressed in rags. They ran to meet the visitors bearing bowls of flowers and ushered them to the palace of the Mir, which was a simple building like a farmhouse. The Mir proudly showed them his two prize possessions, symbols of his power: a telephone that did not work and a piano so badly out of tune that it could not be played. Such poverty was a far cry from the paradise portrayed by James Hilton.

The camera technician said he was terribly let down until he suddenly realized something about these people —they were happy. In all Shangri-La he saw not a single worried face; but he saw many faces wrinkled with smiles. Now he tells people about the lesson the learned there: Shangri-La is a state of mind.[7]

Jesus would say—did say—it's a state of spirit: "Happy are the poor in spirit, for the kingdom of heaven belongs to them."

Notes

[1] Paul W. Powell, "Joseph: Dealing With Bitterness," *Preaching* 3/6 (May-June, 1988): 30.

[2] Clarence Jordan, *Sermon on the Mount*, Rev. Ed., (Valley Forge: Judson Press, 1952), 17.

[3] Friedich Hauck, "*Ptōchhos*," Gerhard Kittel and Gerhard Friedrich, ed., *Theological Dictionary of the New Testament*, trans. Geoffrey W. Bromiley (Grand Rapids: William B. Eerdmans, 1968), Vol. 6, 886.

[4] Calvin Miller, *The Table of Inwardness* (Downers Grove, IL: Inter-Varsity Press, 1984), 48.

[5] Beverly Terrell, told in a seminar at Central Baptist Church, Johnson City, Tennessee, April, 1989.

[6] William Barclay, *The Beatitudes and The Lord's Prayer for Everyman* (New York: Harper and Row, 1963), 28.

[7] Leonard Griffith, *Illusions of our Culture* (Waco: Word Books, 1969), 100–101.

Chapter Three

To Beam or Not to Beam?

Matthew 5:16 vis-à-vis 6:1

by Frank Stagg

As a parody on Hamlet's famous soliloquy, two injunctions within the Sermon on the Mount may be heard as saying: "To beam or not to beam?" What are we to do with our light, let it shine that others may see it or conceal it in the privacy of piety? On the surface and taken literally, Matthew 5:16 and 6:1 may seem to put us under conflicting claims. Is this actual anomaly or the creative tension of polar claims?

A study of Matthew 5:16 vis-a-vis 6:1 is important for an understanding of the Sermon on the Mount; but it also offers light on the nature of the Bible, the nature of language, and biblical hermeneutics.

Hamlet's dilemma left him seeking for a *tertium quid* that was not to be found: "To be or not to be, that is the question." Disillusioned about life when his mother and uncle conspired to murder his father, Hamlet no longer wanted "to be." Never having died and with death to him an unknown, he was afraid "not to be." By contrast, the Sermon on the Mount seems to bind us to both, to beam our light and not to beam it.

Paul's options awaiting trial as he wrote Philippians are happy ones: "For to me, to live is Christ and to die is gain"

(1:21). To die or to live were both positive challenges. The seeming anomaly in the Sermon on the Mount is more nearly a paragon alongside Paul (both options desirable) with little if anything in common with Hamlet (neither option desired). To Beam or not to Beam?

Matthew 5:16

The imperative is firm: "Thus let your light shine before people in order *that they may see your good works* and glorify your Father in heaven." In fact, verses 14-15 rule out as an impossibility that our "light" not shine. By nature, light cannot but shine.

"You are the light of the world" is addressed to "the crowds" who went up a mountain to hear Jesus (Matt 5:1). These people were not a careful selection of religious elites. They were ordinary people.

Probably echoed in Jesus' declaration of these followers as "the light of the world" was the preposterous claim of a semi-monastic group at Qumran that they were "the sons of light." One of the Dead Sea Scrolls is known as "The War between the Sons of Light and the Sons of Darkness." The self-styled "sons of light" at Qumran were hiding their professed light as they awaited one or two messiahs (one a Davidic warrior and the other a priestly presider) who would give them victory over the "sons of darkness" (Romans and others).

Jesus declared the impossibility of light not shining, likening it to a city set upon a mountain. He did not say that such a city should not be hidden but that it cannot be hidden. It is in the nature of light that it must give light.

Perceiving that light is God's gift to people who are "the light of the world," Jesus declared that God's intention in giving light is that it shine. He appealed to the practice of people in lighting a lamp. They *do not* light a lamp and then place it under a basket (unless arson is the motive!). They place the lighted lamp upon a stand so that it may give light to all in the house. We are light only if God has made us light, and God does not light lamps in order to hide their light.

Behind the command that we let our light shine is Jesus' appeal both to light's inherent nature to give light and God's purpose in giving us light. Light is to shine. It is light's nature and light's purpose "to beam."

The motive proper to letting one's light shine is that others "may see your good works and glorify your Father in heaven." Light serves but is not self-serving. As "the light of the world," we are to live in open goodness before other people that they may have the light and that God may be glorified.

Matthew 6:1

"Take heed not to do your righteousness before other people to be seen by them, otherwise you have not reward with your Father in heaven." On the surface, this seems to reverse the command that we so beam our light that other people may see our good works (5:16). Of course, motive is the decisive factor determining whether our being seen is unselfish servanthood or egocentric self-serving.

The tension between 6:1 and 5:16 is heightened by the extensive pursuit of three expressions of piety: almsgiving, prayer, and fasting (6:2-18). These seem to offer no option to privacy or secrecy in almsgiving, prayer, and fasting. In acts of mercy, the left hand is not to know what the right hand is doing (6:3). Alms are to be offered "in secret," seen alone by "your Father." When we pray, it is to be in one's private room with the door closed, God alone seeing it (6:6). Fasting is not to be apparent to other people but known to God alone (6:17).

The popular claim that we are to take the Bible "just as it is" breaks down here as elsewhere. To be taken seriously, the

Bible is to be taken *intentionally* but not literally. In fact, language as such requires that it not be taken literally. When the label reads "Take *one tablet* three times daily," we know that we are not to swallow and regurgitate the same tablet three times a day! We understand that we are to take *three tablets* per day, one at a time. When the psalmist says, "The Lord is my shepherd," we take this analogically and not literally. When Jesus says of a loaf of bread, "This is my body," we take it seriously but not literally.

Creative Tension

There is no actual anomaly between the intention of Matthew 5:16 and 6:1. This does not follow *a priori* from blind dogma which says that there cannot be conflicting perspectives or mutually exclusive commands within the Bible. There are in fact passages in the Bible which oppose other passages, some of the most explicit within the Sermon on the Mount itself. If 5:16 and 6:1 are both valid, as held here, it is not on dogmatic grounds but because they may be found so in terms of problems with which they are concerned and the intention behind each command.

At the heart of the Sermon on the Mount are six "antitheses" in which Jesus corrected or even reversed some former "hearings" from biblical writings. Most emphatic is the reversal in the fifth antitheses, "You have heard that it was said, 'an eye for an eye and a tooth for a tooth,' but I say to you . . ." (5:38f). The formula for retaliation appears in three books of the Torah (Exod 21:24; Lev 24:20; Deut 19:31), and Jesus rejected and reversed this *lex talionis* (so also by implication such scorched earth policies as commanded in such passages as Num 21:35; 31:17f, 32f, Deut 2:34; 3:3-7; 7:1f; 20:13-18; Ps 137:8f). Jesus' rejection of all kosher food laws and the superficial holiness code upon which they were built (Mark 7:1-23) is further evidence that some scriptures require the rejection of others.

A Canon Within a Canon

The protest that we are not to have "a canon within a canon" is a refusal to acknowledge reality. Even those otherwise competent scholars who intend to overcome "a canon within a canon" fall into the trap of employing their won canon within a canon, for they carefully select passages congenial to their method! No follower of Jesus can assimilate to that one's faith or practice such passages as cited above from Torah.

All of us have a canon within a canon. Jesus himself had a canon within a canon. We all "pick and choose" our texts. We differ only in what we choose and how we do it. To some of us, the Lordship of Jesus over all, including Scripture, is basic to our hermeneutics. We do not know fully the mind of Jesus, but we have enough of his way and teaching to guide us in working through diverse or even competing perspectives in the Bible.

Polar Claims

Polar claims, both valid, confront us in Matthew 5:16 and 6:1. These passages claim us from opposite sides, but the tension they impose may be creative, not contradiction or impasse. It is the nature and function of light to give light, so we are to live in open goodness before other people. There is a human tendency to make a show of what we consider to be our virtues, and such inclinations are to be suppressed.

Our good works are to be done openly before others for their good and God's glory, but they are not to be paraded for our own glory. We are to live in open goodness without ostentation.

Even the prescription of privacy does not necessarily solve the problem of showmanship. Even within the privacy of a room with the door closed, we may yet have two audiences: God and ourselves. We may give alms, pray, or fast to impress God; and we may do so to impress ourselves. Only the integrity of love, devotion, and servanthood free us from the self-serving disposition to make a show of our piety. Of course, the self-serving principle may be at work even when one seeks always to conceal good works.

To beam one's light is inherently right, for it is the nature of light to give light. Not to beam one's light is not inherently right, but it may be situationally right, as an effort not to show off one's goodness or piety.

The Ultimate Resolution

The ultimate victory in openly letting our light shine and in doing our good works before others comes when we no longer think in terms of either revealing or concealing our light or our good works. There are moments, at least, in which something of this is attained by many of Jesus' followers. It happens sometimes in crisis situations when we act out of who and what we are, totally for the good of someone else and with no thought even as to whether we are seen or not seen.

Such freedom from the thought of being seen or not seen occurs, for example, when another is in danger and we intervene for that one's safety. Under the urgency of the situation, all that matters is that we act in terms of the other's need. The thought that we may be seen or not seen does not even enter into the action. Ideally, what thus occurs when we are at our best should characterize us normally and not just on occasion. That is the ideal arising out of the polar claims of 5:16 and 6:1.

Chapter Four

The Antitheses Updated

Matthew 5: 21–48 (Paraphrased)

by J. Estill Jones

You have heard that it was said:
>   Thou shalt confess the truth
>   by agreeing to the confession of faith
>   and accepting without question
>   its interpretation by your leaders.

But I say unto you:
>   Live the truth and love the world
>   as God loves the world.
>   Do not seek to intimidate another to your position.
>   Speak the truth in love as you understand it.
>   Encourage both supervisors and subordinates
>   freely to approach God,
>   his will,
>   and his truth
>   for themselves.
>   And love them even when they disagree with you.
>   Talk and pray about your differences,
>   but do not be harshly judgmental,
>   and pray for them
>   if they should become judgmental.

You have heard that it was said:
> Thou shalt love thy nation and hate its enemies.

But I say unto you:
> Love your enemy nations.
> Pray for Russia, Cuba, Bulgaria, Nicaragua, China.
> Share with them the good news of God's love.
> Work for fair and just treaties.
> Receive their visiting nationals.
> Visit their shores.
> Carefully analyze you nation,
>> its system of justice,
>> its standards of honesty,
>> its spokesmen in leadership.
>
> Act responsibly as a Christian citizen
>> . . .think
>> . . . talk.

You have heard that it was said:
> Thou shalt feed thy family and friends
> and insist that the rest of the world do likewise.

But I say unto you:
> If the world hungers,
>> feed it.
>
> If the world thirsts,
>> make it possible for water to flow.
>
> If the Eastern Bloc or the Third World
>> suffers from drought or famine,
>>> share your grain,
>>> share your cattle,

even if prices for bread and milk are raised at
home,
even if they speak unkindly of your economic
system.
If the street people or the welfare families
ask for help,
do not judge their joblessness,
but minister to their needs.

You have heard that it was said:
Thou shalt not lay a wager on the horse race,
nor on the dog race,
nor on the ball game,
nor even at bingo.

But I say unto you:
Work with your hands,
that you may support your family
with honest toil
and earn enough to share
with those who are covetous.
Strive for economic and social justice,
which will make the temptation to get
something for nothing less powerful.
Be absolutely honest yourself,
and model the role of truthfulness
with your tithe,
with you taxes.
Encourage your church to pay fair and adequate
salaries to staff members.
Live within your income.

You have heard that it was said:
> Thou shalt not wage war
>> nor deal violently with any man.

But I say unto you:
> Defend the weak and oppressed
>> against the strong that oppress them.
> Insomuch as possible live peaceably
>> with all men and women.
> Make your home a center for peace
>> among its members
>> and with its neighbors.
> Yet peace is more than the absence of war
>> or the absence of violence.
> So strive for wholeness and health
>> in your relationships.
> And seek to guarantee peace in the nation
>> and among the nations
>>> by giving yourself to justice
>>> and mercy
>>> and love.

You have heard that it was said:
> Thou shalt not violate the law,
>> but thou shalt be just and upright
>> in all thy dealings.

But I say unto you:
> Many expressions of the law are unjust
>> in certain circumstances,
>> with certain persons.
> Add mercy to your expression of justice.

Remember that God forgives
    and you will forgive also.
Protect those who are unjustly
    or unmercifully treated.
Work for laws which are just
    and resist those which are unjust.
Remember that justice and righteousness
    are closely related
       —that God's righteousness is your salvation.

You have heard that it was said:
    "Cursed be Ham, son of Noah"
       —God has determined their appointed sea-
          sons and the bounds of their habitation
       —let them stay in their place.

But I say unto you:
    The earth is the Lord's and the fullness thereof
       —the world and they that dwell therein
       —all folks are made in the image of God.
    There is not one poor and one rich,
    there is not one male and one female,
    there is not one black and one white
       —or red or yellow.
          God loves us all equally.
    Now you act like God
       and love all races equally, too.
    And if you see some person mistreated or neglected,
       go to that person in a spirit of Christian love.
    And welcome all persons to worship
       and Bible study
       and prayer meeting.
    For God so loved the world . . .

You have heard that it was said:
> "The man is the head of the house"
>> —"let the women keep silence in the church."

But I say unto you:
> That he who created man
>> created woman also.
>
> That marriage is to bring man and woman
>> together as equals
>>> —not for one to be the slave
>>> or the property of the other.
>
> That the church exists and is edified
>> by the exercise of the gifts of its members,
>> both male and female.
>
> Therefore, you work for equal opportunity,
>> for fair treatment,
>> for mutual consideration and respect.
>
> And if a woman or a girl is harassed
>> or mistreated
>> or intimidated
>
> —you who are strong and spiritual,
>> help that person,
>> resist the oppressor,
>> and show your acceptance of the principle:
>>> "God so loved the world. . . ."

You have heard that it was said:
> Thou shalt respect the rights of all.

But I say unto you:
> Secure and preserve human rights
>> by personal courage and integrity.

Interpret and defend human rights
    not only in this democracy,
but encourage through the political process
    human rights all over the world.
And in your personal relationships
    let there be no discrimination on your part
        on the basis of sex
        or race
        or economic ability
        or cultural lag
        or educational attainment
        or any other basis.
Know that all men and women are created
    in the image of God
    —persons for whom Christ died.

You have heard that it was said:
    Thou shalt not lust after one of the same sex
        and no homosexual can share
        in the kingdom of God.

But I say unto you:
    Do not lust after any other person,
        for such unholy desires degrade
            the other person
        and subject you to uncontrolled appetites.
    Do not judge harshly one
        whom you do not understand.
            Before God he or she stands or falls.
    Love him or her into normal relationships,
        but love him or her nevertheless.
    Be a friend and an example of wholeness.

You have heard that it was said:
> Thou shalt not waste thy time with television.

But I say unto you:
> Thou shalt not waste thy time with anything!
> Choose wisely the television programs you watch
> . . . balance your programming.
> Exercise Christian stewardship of the on/off button
> with respect to family viewing.
> Do not allow television to substitute
> either for conversation
> or for reading.
> Discuss with family members
> the programs to be viewed
> and then continue the discussion
> concerning the programs viewed.
> Protest indecent programs.
> Promote wholesome programs.
> If the opportunity arises,
> produce worthy programs.
> But do not waste your time with television.

You have heard that it was said:
> Thou shalt not use addictive drugs,
> nor provide them to your child
> or your neighbor's child.

But I say unto you:
> Avoid the very appearance of evil.
> Take medication only when necessary.
> Have nothing to do with the sale or distribution
> of harmful drugs . . .

and where possible use your influence to halt
such distribution
or sale
or use anywhere in the world.
Teach the young and the old the danger
of using drugs.
If they need a high,
let them be filled with the Holy Spirit.
It is more lasting and vastly safer.

You have heard that it was said:
Thou shalt hate your family for my sake
and the gospel's.

But I say unto you:
The good news of the gospel calls for you to love
all men and women and boys and girls
because God loves them all.
Devotion to the Lord God begins with the family
God gave you.
You must provide for their physical needs.
You must love them
and in so doing love God.
The neglect or the break-up of the family
is not a part of God's original plan.
Therefore strive to preserve it.
Accept responsibility to guide its members
into God's will.
Let your family be so closely-knit
that others will recognize your home
as the dwelling place of God.

You have heard that it was said:
>Thou shalt not drink wine or beer
>>or any alcoholic beverage,
>and he who does so has no part
>>in the kingdom of God.

But I say unto you:
>A part of the harvest of the Spirit is self-control
>>. . . and that your body is a temple of the
>>Holy Spirit is clearly stated.
>Be moderate in all things.
>If you see a person prostituted
>>to the greed of another
>>or to the lust of another,
>>>help that person.
>If you see a person blamed
>>or disgraced by over-indulgence in alcohol,
>>>help that person
>>>. . . be a friend.
>If you see a young person tempted
>>to over-indulge in alcohol,
>>>give that young person a helping hand,
>>>>a shoulder to lean on,
>>>>and a solid friendship.
>Encourage parents and other adults
>>to set a good example of self-control.
>Treat your own body as a temple of the Holy Spirit.

Chapter Five

Why Listen to Jesus?
The Legitimation of Jesus
as Interpreter of God's Will[1]

Matthew 5:17–20

by David B. Howell

Matthew 5:17–20 is an important unit of sayings in the Sermon of the Mount for it serves as the programmatic introduction not only to the antitheses but to the rest of the Sermon which follows. The vast number and wide variety of interpretations of Matthew 5:17–20 suggest that these may be some of the most perplexing sayings in Matthew.

My procedure in this essay will be to offer responses to questions which have been raised by these verses before concluding with a brief summary of my line of interpretation. These verses will be examined in terms of their meaning in Matthew since they are found in the context of the Sermon on the Mount, the first of the five great discourses of Jesus's teaching in the Gospel.

I have deliberately chosen the word "response" to characterize my answers to these questions because the issues raised are complex and a variety of "answers" have been given to the questions. In my responses I try to acknowledge the diversity of approaches to the questions, and it remains for the reader to decide if my responses truly answer the questions.

Q. What does Jesus mean when he says that he has come "to fulfill the law and the prophets (5: 17)?"

Interpreters have generally followed one of two broad lines of interpretation when interpreting Jesus's saying about fulfilling the law and the prophets in 5:17: it is understood in a salvation-historical or prophetic sense in which Jesus is the one promised in Scripture who comes to bring God's salvation[2] or it is understood in an ethical sense in which Jesus is the one who obediently keeps and teaches God's will.[3] To understand this saying it is crucial that we understand Matthew's meaning of the verb "fulfill" and the phrase "the law and the prophets."

Scholars who see a prophetic note in "fulfill" in 5:17 usually emphasize that of the sixteen occurrences of "fulfill" in Matthew, twelve of them are found in the Old Testament fulfillment quotations (e.g. Matt 1:22, "to fulfill what the Lord had spoken by the prophet"). Moreover, Jesus's coming does not refer narrowly to the law, but to the prophets as well. One commentator thus translates the phrase "the law and the prophets" as "Scriptures" since the phrase " was a way to refer to the Scriptures in Judaism, in order to emphasize the prophetic force of the saying."[4] Others point out that Matthew can see the whole question of law in light of prophetic fulfillment.[5] In Matthew 11:13 one thus finds the unusual statement "all the prophets and the Law prophesied until John" (cf. Luke 16:16 where the parallel reads "The Law and the prophets lasted until John"). It is unusual first because the saying reverses the normal order of "law and prophets," in effect "standing the accepted canon of the Old Testament on its head."[6] And second, it is unusual to have the noun "law" function as the subject to the verb "prophecy." The result drives home the point that both the law and the prophets pointed ahead to the coming Messiah.

Scholars who follow the second line of interpretation and understand 5:17 primarily in an ethical sense argue that the prophetic interpretation overlooks both the antithetical pairing of "to abolish/to fulfill" in the saying and its context in Matthew prior to the antitheses in vv. 21–48. The parallelism between the two verbs suggests that Jesus fulfills the law and prophets by his obedient practice or doing of the demands of the law and prophets. This seems to be the sense of "fulfill" in 3:15, the closest parallel to Matthew's use of "fulfill" in 5:17, when Matthew speaks of Jesus and John doing what God demands ("fulfill all righteousness") in Jesus's baptism.

To read these two verses in light of Matthew's more normal usage of "fulfill" in the Old Testament fulfillment quotations may be to minimize the difference between the passive form of the verb used in the fulfillment quotations and the active form in 3:15 and 5:17. Those who follow this ethical line of interpretation of 5:17 also believe that Matthew was thinking of the demands of the prophets in the phrase "the law and the prophets." The use of this phrase in Matthew 7:12 and 22:40 definitely gives it a particular normative nuance as it is used there in ethical exhortations. More specifically, it is the prophetic message of mercy and love which provide a principle for interpreting the demands of the law (22:40; cf. Matt 9:13 and 12:7 where Jesus uses Hos 6:6 in disputes with the scribes and Pharisees).

I personally believe that what I have labeled the ethical line of interpretation, which sees Jesus fulfilling the law and prophets through his obedient deeds and teaching of God's will, is closer to Matthew's understanding of the saying in 5:17. The two lines of interpretation are not mutually exclusive, however, because Jesus is able to do and proclaim the demands of God precisely because he is the promised

Messiah. The phrase "I have come" is used throughout the gospels to describe the mission of one who comes to bring God's salvation to humanity and reverse expectations people have of his mission (cf. Matt 10:34 which closely parallels the form of our saying here: "Do not think I have come to bring peace to earth; I have not come to bring peace but a sword"). Matthew's use of "fulfill" indirectly points at Jesus's person and role as God's agent of salvation because he reserves this term for Jesus alone, using "to do" or "to observe" to refer to disciples's acts of obedience (cf. 28:19–29).

Q. What do "iota" and "dot" refer to in 5:18?

The two words refer to small letters or details of Hebrew writing. *Iota* is a Greek word translating the Hebrew *yod,* which is the smallest Hebrew letter. "Dot" refers to an ornamental hook or accent mark in Hebrew. These words taken together with the phrase "until heaven and earth pass away," which can be understood as either a colorful Jewish way of saying "never" or as referring to the apocalyptic consummation of this age, affirm the enduring character of the law in its smallest detail. One commentator helps explain its meaning by looking at its parallel in Luke 16:17. Here it precedes the prohibition on divorce (5:18), and Hendrickx argues that the word *iota* (even though it is not in Luke) helps explain the connection between the two sayings in the Aramaic tradition.

A rabbinical text runs as follows:

> Who accused Solomon? Rabbi Jehoshua ben Levi said: "The *yod* in *yarbeh.*" Rabbi Simeon ben Jokai taught: "The Book of Deuteronomy ascended into heaven, prostrated before God and said: 'Lord of the world, You have written in your Law: "Each testament of which one prescription is violated is totally violated." Behold Solomon seeks to destroy a *yod* of mine.' And God answered: 'Solomon and a thousand

like him will pass away but no single word/stroke/*yod* of your's shall pass.'"

There can be no doubt that this text refers to Deuteronomy 17:17 which reads: *lo's yarbeh-lo nashim*, "he (the king) shall not multiply his wives for himself." What does to "destroy the *yod* of this law" mean? Omitting the *yod* of this law one gets: *lo's arbeh-lo nashim*, "to multiply wives," that is according to this rabbinical interpretation, exactly the opposite.[7]

Q. To what does "until all things come to pass" (5:18) refer?

There are two temporal clauses in this saying about the binding force of the law. This second clause is vague. One approach is to make the two clauses synonymous. The second clause can be understood in terms of the first and thus also refers to the end of history (cf. Matt 24:34), or the first clause can be understood in terms of the second. If this option is followed, scholars point to the parallels between this phrase and some of the Old Testament fulfillment quotations (Matt 1:22; 21:4) and argue that the binding force of law is valid until Jesus's coming which culminates in his death and resurrection.

Another approach is to make the second clause explanatory of the first. That is to say, the second clause explains how the law remains valid until the end. Emphasis here is also put on Christ's work of doing and teaching what God demands; "law" now means law as it is interpreted and taught by Jesus. This approach has the strength of resolving the tension between the affirmation of the Law's permanent nature and Jesus's handling of the Old Testament in the antitheses which follow.[8]

It seems to me that both approaches to interpreting 5:18 have the effect of qualifying the affirmation of the permanence of the law. Jesus's coming, his actions and his teaching, reshapes people's understanding of what God demands. It is interesting to note that while Jesus affirms the validity or authority of the Old Testament here, this saying seems to me to say nothing about some doctrine of inerrancy as it is sometimes used. The antitheses which follow make it clear that the Old Testament is not the supreme and absolute criteria of authority. Jesus goes beyond it and for the Christian becomes his/her authority and norm.

Q. Matthew 5:19 talks about the "least of the commandments." Where are the commandments ranked?

The phrase probably refers to debates in contemporary Judaism among rabbis between "light" (unimportant) and "heavy" (important) commandments. The verb "to loose/relax" when referring to commandments means to repeal or annul. It is interesting to note here that Matthew characteristically connects doing with saying or teaching. If the saying was directed to "official" teachers in the church, it still does not exempt every disciple from being consistent in word and deed (cf. 7:21ff.). While "commandment" usually refers to individual Old Testament commandments (15:3; 19:17; 22:36,38,40), Matthew can also use its corresponding verb "to command" with Jesus's demands (28:20). Other connections between the Great Commission (28:18–20) and 5:17–20 (e.g. teaching, "to observe," "to do," and "all") have led some to suggest that the commandments in 5:19 that are to be taught and obeyed could also be understood as Christ's own teaching which the Christian is now to obey.[9]

Q. What does Matthew mean by the phrase "Kingdom of heaven?"

The phrase is synonymous with "Kingdom of God." The word "heaven" is a Jewish circumlocution for saying the name of God, the "heavens" are the abode of God. In Jesus's teaching it is usually taken to mean God's rule or sovereignty. In Matthew 5:19–20 the expression seems to refer to future rule of God, but it also has a present sense; God's rule is tied to Jesus's ministry and, in some sense, is present for the Christian.

Q. To what does "righteousness" refer?

"Righteousness" in Matthew does not have the Pauline sense of "standing in right relationship to God." Rather, it is used by Matthew in the ethical sense of conduct which is in obedient conformity to the will of God. The correspondence between righteousness and doing the will of God is nowhere more evident than in 5:20 and 7:21. The parallels between these two sayings in the Sermon about entering the Kingdom suggest that righteousness and doing the will of God the Father are closely related concepts. When taken together, they form an overarching and encompassing description of the character and conduct of a disciple.

Q. Matthew 5:20 suggests that scribes and Pharisees were righteous. I did not think they were?

Matthew does not deny that righteousness can be predicated to the Jewish leaders in 5:20, rather the point of the saying is that their righteousness is insufficient for entrance into the Kingdom. If righteousness is conduct in conformity to the will of God, the righteousness of the Pharisees must be conduct which is in conformity to the will of God as it has been revealed in the Law and the prophets. Matthew makes a distinction between the righteousness of the disciples and the righteousness of the scribes and Pharisees, however, which reveals both continuity and discontinuity in the disciples's righteousness. The continuity can be seen in the use of the same word, "righteousness," to describe both groups as well as in the affirmation that Jesus has come to fulfill rather than abolish the Law and the prophets (5:17).

The use of the words "greater" and "exceed" in 5:20 discloses the discontinuity. This discontinuity has both a quantitative and qualitative sense. It is a mistake if one assumes that this greater righteousness is to be located in a more strict and meticulous observance of the law. Such an interpretation ignores the force of 5:17, which states that Jesus is the eschatological fulfiller of the Law in his life and teaching, and the close connection between righteousness and the Kingdom which Matthew makes (5:10, 20; 6:33; 21:31–2). The greater righteousness of the disciples is therefore to be located in obedience to Jesus's teaching which is now normative for the disciples.

Our understanding of the disciples's greater righteousness is clarified by Matthew's use of the word "perfection" in 5:48 and 19:21. In the story of the rich young man the quantitative element of perfection is plainly directed to discipleship and obedience to Jesus. The young man has apparently kept all the commandments—Jesus does not criticize the man's confession of obedience—but the extra needed by the man is obedience to Jesus, indicated in this pericope by the demand to sell all his possessions. The obedience demanded is nothing less than the call for total commitment and whole-heartedness which is issued to all potential disciples. This pericope now makes Matthew's use of perfection in 5:48 clear for perfection is the same as the greater righteousness needed to enter the Kingdom (5:20).

The notion of perfection applies to all the antitheses in 5:21–48 as Jesus interprets the Law in his teaching. The righteousness and perfection of the disciples is realized in obedient conformity to the norm of God's will as revealed in Jesus's teaching. The qualitative distinction of the disciples's righteousness and perfection is derived from the fact that they are grounded in the teaching of Jesus who is the eschatological fulfiller of the Law and the one who makes the new relationship with God possible. This prevents the greater righteousness of the disciples from simply being a more meticulous, legalistic observance of the Law. Obedience is realized in the context of a relationship with God which Jesus makes possible.

SUMMARY

It now remains for me to summarize how I understand the flow of thought in Matthew 5:17–20. This pericope serves as the programmatic introduction to the teaching which follows. It is programmatic first because it establishes Jesus as the eschatological and authoritative interpreter of the Law and the prophets (5:17-18), and secondly because it explicitly characterizes the conduct demanded of the disciples (5:19 –20). The normative nuance which the phrase "the Law and the prophets: is given by the evangelist in his gospel suggests that the emphasis in 5:17 is more broadly placed than an interpretation which understands Jesus as the salvation-historical fulfillment of Scripture. Rather, Matthew wishes to stress that the will of God which had been expressed in the Law and the prophets is not revealed and interpreted in Jesus's teaching and actions. This is underlined throughout the Gospel as the Matthean Jesus speaks confidently in many of the controversy stories with his opponents about the behavior and attitudes God desires. He frequently cites the Old Testament in support of his action and position, pointing out how his opponents have misunderstood or ignored the commands of God (9:13; 11:5,10; 12:7; 13:14ff.; 15:7ff.; 19:5, 18ff.; 21:13,16,42; 22:32,44; 26:31). Matthew is able to stress the permanently binding character of Jesus's teaching because Jesus makes known the will of God (cf. 28:20). The greater righteousness of the disciples therefore means conformity to God's will as it had been revealed in Jesus's teaching and actions. The quantitative and qualitative difference between this righteousness and that of the scribes and Pharisees is to be found in obedience to Jesus whether his teaching be understood as completing, replacing, adding to, or radicalizing the demands of God expressed in the Law and the prophets. With all of these possible interpretations, the content of this righteousness is explicated in the teaching which follows.

At what is essentially the beginning of Jesus's teaching ministry, Matthew 5:17–20 thus functions to place Jesus clearly at the center of the Christian's morality. Jesus's teaching is emphasized in the immediate context, but his actions cannot be divorced from his teaching. When Jesus's listeners are confronted with the demands of discipleship throughout the Gospel, they are also confronted with Jesus's actions realizing these demands. In a sense, this pericope legitimates Jesus's role as a model for discipleship in the Gospel. It is because Jesus is the eschatological fulfiller of the Law and the prophets and the revealer of God's will that he is exemplary for the disciples.

Notes

[1]In appreciation to the Blanton Sunday School class at Second Baptist Church, Liberty, Missouri—not only for providing the questions for this study, but for being a congenial fellowship where one can ask questions when studying the Bible.

[2]See Herman Hendrickx, *The Sermon on the Mount* (London: Chapman, 1984) 45ff. or Robert A. Guelich, *The Sermon on the Mount* (Waco: Word, 1982) 138–43, 162–64 for representatives of this line of interpretation.

[3]See Ulrich Luz, *Das Evangelium nach Matthäus* (Mt. 1–7), EKK (Zurich: Benziger Verlag, 1985) 228–44 or Eduard Schweizer, *The Good News according to Matthew* (Atlanta: John Knox Press, 1975) 107 for representatives of this line of interpretation.

[4]Guelich 163–64.

[5]John P. Meier, *The Vision of Matthew* (New York: Paulist, 1979) 224–28.

[6]Ibid., 226.

[7]Hendrickx 48.   •

[8]See Guelich, 145–49 for a good discussion of the different ways of interpreting the two temporal clauses in 5:18.

[9]See John P. Meier, *Law and History in Matthew's Gospel* (Rome: Biblical Institute Press, 1976) 123.

Chapter Six

Jesus' Attitude Toward the Law in Matthew 5:17–48

by T. C. Smith

After giving the Beatitudes to illustrate the characteristics of those who submit to the rule of God, and after calling on his disciples to be a preservative element in society as well as a shining light in their righteousness, Jesus clarified his opinion of the Mosaic law. Presumably this was done in order to clear up any misunderstanding about the six antithetical sayings that were to follow. Through the years the preamble to the six contrasts (Matt 5:17–20) has caused many New Testament scholars to raise a number of questions. (1) Did Jesus utter these words, or did Matthew insert them because he was writing to a Jewish Christian community that still upheld the law? (2) If verse 17 is from the lips of Jesus, what did he mean by "fulfill" the law? (3) Is not verse 18 a more stringent view of the Scriptures than that of the Pharisees? (4) Does verse 19 look back to verses 17–18 or forward to the antithetical sayings?

Those who raise the first question maintain that these verses should be excluded from the Sermon on the Mount because they appear to be an invention of Matthew. The material does not occur in Mark, and only verse 18 is found in Luke. On the surface it might seem that Matthew has taken these verses from Q, a source used by both Matthew and Luke, but Luke chose to record only one of the verses in 16:17. A close scrutiny, however, shows that verse 18 is not the equivalent of Luke 16:17. Therefore Matthew is alone in the recording of the preamble to the six contrasts.

The second question pertains to the meaning of 5:17. If Jesus did not abrogate the law and the prophets, what did he mean by fulfilling them? The Greek word for fulfill (*pleroō*) has a variety of meanings. It means (1) to complete in detail; (2) to cause to stand and confirm the true meaning; (3) to make true what has been said or promised; (4) to establish; (5) to fill up in measure. There would be no difficulty in understanding what Jesus said concerning fulfilling the law and prophets if verses 18–19 had not been inserted. These verses make Jesus take a more literalistic stand on the law than the Pharisees. To be sure Jesus upheld certain portions of the law, but it is very clear from the illustrations which follow in the contrasts that he did not support or endorse the literalistic interpretations of the law espoused by the Pharisees.

Of the meanings given to *pleroō* it seems that "establish" is most accurate in this context. Some scholars believe that the Aramaic word *kâyyêm* is the reason for the use of this Greek word. *Kâyyêm* means "to establish or to uphold." In a second century CE. Midrash (commentary) on Exodus Rabbi Pappias said, "Man has become as one of us" (Gen 3:22).[1] He interpreted this to signify that God likens man to angels. His contemporary Rabbi Akiba rejected the opinion of Pappias. As a consequence Pappias replied, "How then do you uphold (*kâyyêm*) this verse?" Akiba abruptly responded, "Man has become one of two ways, the evil one of his choice." The Hebrew text of Genesis 3:22 has *mimmennu* (of us) though it could also be *mimmennō* (of himself). Akiba used *mimmennō* and consequently upheld his doctrine of the evil and good impulses by exchanging the place of a dot on the Hebrew *waw*.

How did Jesus uphold the law and the prophets, if in three of the antithetical sayings he did, in fact, invalidate the law? Jesus began where the law stood, but he brought out the spirit of the law by stressing the intention of God behind the letter. He chose to go beyond the scribal minutiae and affirmed the genuine will of God by expressing his own insights. Jesus dared to make a distinction between the will of God and the expression of that will in the law. Paul in Romans 3:31 contends before his imaginary objectors that he upholds the law. Admittedly another Greek word is used, but it is equivalent to the rabbinic *kâyyêm*. How does he establish the law? He accomplishes this by using one of Hillel's principles of interpretation known as the *gezera shava* and in turn reversing the *gezera shava*. By this method he proves that a right relationship with God had always been on the basis of faith.

Is verse 18 more stringent than the opinion of the Pharisees toward Scripture? It certainly appears to be. The saying preserves the permanent validity of the law to the very letter. Shall we accuse Jesus of being a literalist? Yet on the other hand he taught contrary to certain portions of the law. Could this be another hyberbole of Jesus like "a camel going through the eye of a needle," or "straining out the gnat and swallowing a camel?" It is possible that he had reference to the Torah (law) as divine instruction rather than the multitude of community rules or rituals of the Pentateuch and rabbinic oral tradition. If so, Jesus was concerned less for each little precept and more interested in the essential core which did have permanent validity.

It would be to our advantage to know the context in which verse 18 was originally delivered, rather than depend upon Matthew's arbitrary collection of materials that make up the Sermon on the Mount. We have already noted that Luke contains a similar saying, but there are some differences as well (16:17). If we could say that there was some sort of continuity in Luke 16, though this is very difficult to affirm, the immediate context of Luke 16:17 is a denunciation of the Pharisees by Jesus. Therefore, Jesus was condemning the stringency of the scribes with respect to Scripture and was not supporting the permanency of the law when he said, "But it is easier for heaven and earth to pass away, than for one dot of the law to fall?"(v. 17)

Does verse 19 look back to verses 17–18 or forward to the antithetical sayings? Are the commandments in verse 19 equivalent to law in the previous verses? The grammatical structure favors the commands which follow rather than the commandments in verses 17 and 18. The writer should have used "those" instead of "these" if his reference was to the previous verses. Over 60 years ago Montefiore, the famous Jewish scholar, made a very helpful suggestion.[2] He proposed the possibility of verses 19 and 20 being originally another contrast. The antithesis would run like this, "Whoever abrogates one of the smallest commands in the law shall be called least in the kingdom of heaven, and whoever does and teaches them shall be called greatest in the kingdom of heaven, but I say to you that unless your righteousness excels that of the scribes and Pharisees. . . ." Montefiore's observation is indeed very fascinating, but we have no manuscript evidence to support the conclusion. It seems to me if there was an antithesis here, it would take in verses 18–20.

In the conclusion to the preamble to the six contrasts Jesus said, "For I tell you, unless your righteousness exceeds that of the scribes and Pharisees, you will never enter the kingdom of heaven" (v. 20). Probably the most religious men who ever lived were the Pharisees. They were very conscientious in trying to follow the commands of God. They were strict observers of the most minute details of the law. They supposed that this punctiliousness in adhering to God's demands was righteousness. They studied the law so that they would be in close contact with the intention of God, but, sad to say, they never discovered it. Their obedience to God was measurable by deeds which in turn accrued into capital gains. The law became a roof to shelter them from the penetrating light of God's will. God was hidden behind the law, and they concealed themselves from God behind a wall of works and achievements.

Jesus told his disciples that their righteousness must surpass the kind shown by the Pharisees if they wished to be submissive to God's will. What kind of righteousness excels that of the religious leaders of Jesus' day? It is quite clear from the beatitudes and what follows in the Sermon on the Mount the kind of righteousness Jesus had in mind. Genuine righteousness comes from within the individual. It stems from the inner life which has been transformed by the power of God. It is an inner purity of character, and an outward display of that inner purity. The outward manifestation is consistent with the inner character of the person. By submitting to God's sovereignty we display mercy, love, peace, honesty, sincerity, purity, and humility. When we come into contact with society, we are to be what we are in the presence of God.

Verse 20 seems to introduce the reader to the antithetical sayings in chapter five and continues with its emphasis through verse 18 of the sixth chapter. The kind of righteousness that exceeds the righteousness of the Pharisees is seen on the horizontal level of personal relationships in the contrasts that are made. On the vertical level of our relationship with God, we are to excel the Pharisees' religious acts of piety (6:1–18).

The Six Contrasts

All of the antithetical sayings follow more or less this particular pattern, "You have heard it was said by them of old, but I say to you." The first clause gives a scriptural rule narrowly interpreted, and the second clause proposes a wider demand by Jesus. Jesus went back to the spirit and heart of the commandments for his interpretaion.

The rabbis had a formula similar to the one used by Jesus, but it was stated in reverse order. They said, "I might hear or understand the literal meaning in Scripture to be such and such, but you must say." A good example of this form is found in a commentary on Exodus which represents the interpretation of the school of Ishmael in the second century CE In an exposition of the fifth commandment in Exodus 20:12 the rabbis remarked: "I might understand the command to mean honor with words only." They went on to say that Proverbs 3:9 used the same Hebrew word for honor, and in that context the word meant to honor with substance. Thus the rabbis concluded that honor in the fifth commandment also pertained to food, drink, and clothing.

The Pharisees believed that if they kept the text of the law, as interpreted by itself or by tradition, they were accepted by God. This was a limited concept of obedience. When a person obeyed a literal command, he or she could feel secure and pretend to keep the evil desire isolated from himself or herself. In the event that a Jew went beyond what the law proposed, this act of itself earned favor and merit with God.

Jesus refused to accept this scheme of things. He could not tolerate the use of the law as a screen to ward off the fullness of God's revelation. He forced the Jewish leaders to examine their inner life of thoughts, desires, and motives. He taught that God searches us and reveals our wickedness. He destroys our contentment with self and makes up depend completely on the grace and mercy of God.

The rabbis taught that God's judgment depended on what a person did or did not do. Jesus insisted that the ultimate test is the character of the person. While it is true that actions reveal character as Jesus indicated in Matthew 7:16, actions do not reveal all about human nature and disposition. God alone knows this. In each of the antithetical sayings before us, Jesus demanded a radical transformation of character, attitude, and disposition.

The Sanctity of Life

Jesus spoke to the common people who were generally illiterate. The Scriptures were in Hebrew, the language of the scholars. The rabbis read from the Old Testament in Hebrew before the congregation in the synagogue, but they depended on a translator to present the Aramaic paraphrase so the people could understand what was written. Thus it was appropriate for Jesus to say, "You have heard," rather than, "You have read."

The first contrast upholds the sanctity of life. Jesus referred to the sixth commandment of the Decalogue which stressed the sacredness of human life by prohibiting murder (Exod 20:13; Deut 5:17). The latter part of the clause "anyone who murders will be subject to judgment"(v. 21) is based on the written law (Lev 24:17; Deut 17:8–13). "Subject to Judgement" signifies that a person was liable to trial and punishment prescribed by the law. The person charged with murder was brought before the Sanhedrin, the ecclesiastical and civil court of the Jews. If convicted, the accused was put to death.

The Old Testament prophets pronounced their oracles with "thus says the Lord." The Pharisees claimed that they were the successors to the prophets, but they were not so bold to say that they received their authority directly from God. They appealed to the sages, the majority opinion of the rabbis, or their own ordination as a sufficient source of power to make declarations. Theirs was a derived authority. In contrast to the Pharisees Jesus made and declared his decisions on his own authority. Thus he was able to say, "But I tell you."

Jesus went beyond the simple statement of the law's demand to declare the intention of God who gave the commandment. He condemned not only the overt act of murder, but also the inner attitude from which the act originated. He was as much concerned for the causes as he was for the consequences of sinful acts. The courts addressed themselves to the prohibited act which was the end of the process. But Jesus went back to the motivation and thoughts that produced the deed. He considered coddled anger as incipient murder. He said, "Anyone who is angry with his brother will be subject to judgment." The King James Version says, "Whoever is angry with his brother without cause." Without cause "appears in a few reliable manuscripts as well as in quotations from the Fathers. However, the earliest manuscripts do not have this reading. The insertion suggests that a later scribe found the teachings of Jesus too strong for him.

In 1 John 3:15 the author of the epistle undoubtedly was aware of the teaching of Jesus on anger in the Sermon on the Mount when he said, "Anyone who hates his brother is a murderer." Rabbi Eliezer, a teacher of the first century CE was in agreement with Jesus when he said, "He who hates his neighbor, behold, he belongs to the shedders of blood." The kind of anger Jesus was talking about was not a sudden burst of rage that soon exhausted itself. The word used by Matthew is *orgizomenos*, which means a seething type of anger. It is a wrath which is nursed to keep it warm, an anger over which a person broods and will not allow to go away.

The consequence of anger is judgment. What kind of judgment did Jesus have in mind? Some scholars believe that he referred to judgment in the local courts. But the Jewish tribunals, just like the courts today, had no jurisdiction over a person who was angry. They could address themselves only to the overt act produced by anger. The judiciary had no sure way of knowing the inner feelings, thoughts, and motives of a person. There seems to be no doubt that Jesus indicated divine judgment. Only God can properly judge a person's disposition. He alone would have the knowledge needed.

Verses 22b–26 are an expansion of the antithetical statement on murder. The content is closely related to verses

21–22a. Thus the antithesis lies in the contrast between the external act of murder, which is under the jurisdiction of the courts, and the inward disposition which is under the jurisdiction of God. By rabbinic and worldly standards a good person is one who does not commit an overt act to disobey the law. By Jesus' standard no individual is good until the disposition to do what is forbidden is changed. Jesus extended the scope of the law against murder and included within the sweep of its prohibition not only the overt act but the attitude. Murder is not just stabbing, shooting, or poisoning a person. Hatred is a type of murder. The actual deed stems from harboring a bitter resentment, keeping the fires of wrath burning, bearing grudges, and seeking revenge.

In addition to anger Jesus included contempt and abuse. To call a brother a *raka* was a cause for litigation. The person who used this word against someone else was liable to the Sanhedrin, the Jewish court. It is not certain what this Aramaic word signified. Some suppose that it is to be identified with the rabbinic word *reqa*—meaning "good for nothing." At any rate it was an insulting word. Insults under Jewish law were looked upon as downgrading one's humanity. The Sanhedrin declared it mandatory that reparations in money be made to the injured party. Apparently calling a brother a fool was not a basis for litigation in the courts. The word used here in Greek is *more*. In rabbinic literature the Greek word is transliterated as *moreh*, and for the sages it meant "stubborn." Nevertheless, it was some sort of abusive word, and whoever used it against a brother was liable to God's judgment.

It is doubtful that verses 23–26 are a part of the first antithetical saying. The last two verses have a parallel in Luke 12:57–59, but verses 23–24 do not appear in Mark or Luke. Matthew must have decided that these sayings were relevant to the subject at hand. The subject is reconciliation. Jesus declared that reconciliation takes precedence over worship in the Temple. Peaceful relations must be maintained at all costs. If an individual should go to the Temple to present his offering, and there remembers that his brother has feelings against him he is to take the initiative in making peace with his brother before making his offering. In Judaism if a person wronged his neighbor, he must ask forgiveness of the one wronged before God will forgive him. In Jesus' teaching it is the person who is wronged that seeks reconciliation. Rabbi Eleazar ben Azariah, a sage of the second century CE said: "For transgressions that are between man and God the Day of Atonement effects atonement; but for transgressions that are between man and his fellow the Day of Atonement effects atonement only if he has appeased his fellow."[3]

The Sanctity of Marriage

The second contrast is introduced by reciting the seventh commandment of the Decalogue which was a prohibition of adultery (Exod 20:14; Deut 5:18). In Jewish law adultery was sexual intercourse between a married woman and a man other than her husband. The Jews also taught that if a woman was betrothed to a man and had sexual intercourse with a man other than her betrothed, she was guilty of adultery. The rule that applied to the wife did not apply to the husband. In Judaism the husband did not commit adultery against his wife or against a woman to whom he was engaged. The unfaithful husband only committed adultery against his lover's husband.

In verse 28 Jesus supplemented the seventh commandment with the tenth commandment which was against coveting. As in the case of murder, he made a distinction between the overt act of adultery and the inward attitude that produced the act. The law of adultery was given to protect the sanctity of marriage. Jesus expanded the seventh commandment to include lust, and by this addition enhanced the purity of the man-woman relationship. The burning desire of a man to have sexual intercourse with a woman other than his wife shows what kind of person is within. In the eyes of God such a person is an adulterer. The rabbis also declared that lust was a breach of the seventh commandment. They said that if anyone looked at a woman to desire her, he committed unlawful intercourse with her.

While the sin of adultery was specifically limited to those who were married, Jesus seems to include fornication in verse 28 by warning his disciples about the lustful look at any woman. Both adultery and fornication are extreme forms of a desire to violate the personality of another. In love there is recognition of responsibility to correspond to the privilege of sex. In lust there is the desire to use a person selfishly and irresponsibly. Today we speak of viewing someone as a sex object rather than a person in God's image. Love for a person excludes using him/her to pander to one's lust.

Verses 29–30 are similar to Mark 9:43–48 and Matthew 18:8–9. It is quite possible that Matthew decided to incorporate these verses from his dependence on Marcan material and place them after verse 28 because he thought the teaching was relevant to lust. The order in Mark is hand, foot, and eye. Matthew mentions only the eye and the hand, omitting the foot. Matthew seems to connect the eye with the lustful look.

In Judaism the right hand was of greater value than the left hand. By assimilation Matthew gave the same value to the right eye. Sight and touch with the hand stimulate passions. With this rhetorical exaggeration Jesus was telling his disciples that a blemish in any part of the body might contaminate the whole. Sin in any part of the person needs to be conquered before it spreads throughout one's life.

We are not to suppose that the words of Jesus should be taken literally. Very few Christians have done so in the history of the Church. If a person should go so far as to pluck out the right eye, the left eye remains for lustful

looking. The person who cuts off his right hand still possess-
es feeling in the left hand. Even if one is blind, passion has
not been removed. Jesus sought purity in heart, and he
taught that no sacrifice was too great or painful to achieve
this goal.

Divorce

In the third antithetical saying of Jesus the introductory
formula, "You have heard that it was said" is noticeably
abbreviated to simply, "It was said" (v. 31). This contrast has
to do with divorce. The "it was said" is a reference to
Deuteronomy 24:1 which says, "When a man takes a wife
and marries her, if then, she finds no favor in his eyes
because he has found some indecency in her, and he writes
her a bill of divorce and puts it in her hands and sends her
out of the house . . . ." Thus the Deuteronomic code allows
divorce on the basis of some inadequacy or an unseemly
practice.

In the first century CE both groups of Pharisees, the school
of Shammai and the school of Hillel, allowed divorce on the
basis of the teaching of Deuteronomy 24:1. Those who
embraced the view of Shammai were more stringent in their
ruling. For them the grounds for divorce were only in the
case of adultery which they interpreted as an unseemly
practice. Those who followed Hillel were more liberal. Hillel
himself said that a man may divorce his wife "even if she
spoiled a dish for him" (*Mishnah Gittin* 9:10). In the same
reference in the Mishnah we note that Akiba, a rabbi of the
second century CE, said that if a man found a woman more
beautiful than his wife, he had grounds for divorce. As
evidence he quoted that part of Deuteronomy 24:1 that says,
"And it shall be if she finds favor in his eyes."

This saying on divorce attributed to Jesus in the Sermon
on the Mount as parallels in Mark 10:11–12 and Luke 16:18.
The saying of Jesus occurs again in Matthew 19:9f. In both of

the references in Matthew an exception clause has been inserted. For many years this exception clause has been viewed by scholars with great suspicion. It is considered spurious for many reasons. (1) Since Jesus did not give exceptions in other matters but set forth absolutes, it is very doubtful that he did in this instance. (2) Mark and Luke seem to know nothing of divorce allowable for unchastity. (3) Paul in 1 Corinthians 7:10–16 is not aware of the exception clause. (4) In the light of Jesus' total teachings, it does not appear that he would condone divorce on the basis of unlawful sexual intercourse as long as the guilty person asked for forgiveness. (5) In Matthew 19:10 the reply of Jesus' disciples to his teaching on divorce was, "If such is the case of a man with his wife, it is not expedient to marry." This of itself indicates that Jesus set forth the absolute which was no divorce. Otherwise, the disciples would not have been so shocked. (6) Finally, there would be no reason for Jesus to say that Deuteronomy 24:1 was not the intention of God but came in as a concession to the people because previous to the command a wife could be dismissed without a reason and thus violate her rights.

At any rate when the Pharisees in Matthew 19:3 asked Jesus, "Is it lawful to divorce one's wife for any reason?", it is clear that they were trying to put him on the spot to force an agreement with Hillel or Shammai. By inserting the exception clause, the author has put Jesus on the side of Shammai. However, the rest of what Jesus said does not coincide with this opinion. In the remainder of the conversation Matthew follows Mark. The Pharisees wanted to know why Moses permitted divorce. The response of Jesus was that Deuteronomy 24:1 was not the intention of God but a concession on the part of Moses due to the hardness of heart among the Israelites. Up until the time of the Deuteronomic code, a man could tell his wife to hit the road for no reason at all. The implication is that Deuteronomy 24:1 was a protection of the rights of women against capricious men.

Jesus then appealed to Genesis 1:27 and 2:24 to show that it was the intention of God from the very beginning that there should be unity in marriage. To the purpose of God for marriage in the creation accounts, Jesus added, "What therefore God has joined together, man is not to sever" (v. 6). On the basis of what Jesus said here, the exception clause in 19:9 does not coincide at all with the divine intention. This clause reduces the absolute to a relative.

As to the consequences relative to divorce there are some differences between Matthew and Mark. Mark 10:11 has, "Whoever divorces his wife and marries another commits adultery against her." This was not in accord with Jewish law for if a man divorced his wife and married another, he committed adultery against the man who was previously married to her. Never did the Jews consider that a man committed adultery against his wife. In Matthew 5:32 if a man married a divorced woman, he committed adultery. Is it against his divorced wife or against the man who divorced his wife? The text is not clear on this point. Matthew 19:9 does not include marrying a divorced woman, but simply if a man "marries another, he commits adultery." The inference is that the man married a woman who was single. In this case there would be agreement with Mark that the man committed adultery against his divorced wife. Luke is also in agreement with Matthew 19:9 and 5:32b (Luke 16:18).

Matthew 5:32b contains something not in Mark. If a man divorced his wife, he made the wife an adulteress. However, the author added the exception to the rule. If a man's wife was guilty of illicit sexual intercourse, he did not make his wife an adulteress because she was already in that condition. Yet if she was not guilty, the husband through divorce made the woman an adulteress in the eyes of the public. Thus the husband bore the full moral responsibility for the state of affairs of the wife.

In Jewish law the wife was not allowed to divorce her husband, yet Mark has Jesus saying, "If she divorces her

husband and marries another, she commits adultery" (10:12).
It is true that in certain cases a wife could force her husband
to divorce her, but it was never proper in Judaism to say that
a woman could divorce her husband. Admittedly, there were
a few exceptions. We know from the Elephantine papyri that
a Jewish colony in Egypt permitted a wife to divorce her
husband, but this cannot be cited as an orthodox practice in
Judaism because this colony of Jews was unorthodox in the
way that they practiced their religion.

Though there are some discrepancies in the Synoptic
Gospels concerning Jesus' teaching about divorce, the main
issue has to do with the rights of women. In Judaism the
wife was viewed as nothing more than property, and the
husband was in full control. The wife was subjected to the
personal whims, caprices, and vagaries of a kink-in-the-brain
husband. In his teaching on divorce, Jesus emerges as a
champion for the cause of women.

Oaths

The fourth contrast of Jesus is about oaths. The "you have
heard" is not an exact citation of the Old Testament. It is a
conflation or a summary of Leviticus 19:12, Exodus 20:7,
Numbers 30:2f., and Deuteronomy 5:11 and 23:22. All of
these verses are directly or indirectly connected with the
third commandment. The Hebrews were allowed to call upon
God as a witness to assure others that they would complete
their vows and also be truthful in any testimony they gave.
However, they were cautioned to be certain that they fulfilled
their oaths and told the truth; otherwise, their vows meant
nothing and their credibility was questioned. In addition and
this was more sinful, they held little regard for God by
whom they swore. Consequently, the character of God was
dishonored by them.

The rabbis tried to dissuade the Jews from taking an oath
which they could not keep. They also taught that only an

oath was binding when the person swore in the name of God. This gave rise to the Jews taking an oath and circumventing the name of God. They could swear by objects relating to worship such as the Temple, the gold of the Temple, the altar, and heaven. It was a principle of casuistry. But this misled the people into believing that some oaths were not binding. At the same time the evasion gave the vows a sort of religious coloration as though they were binding. By allowing the people to circumvent the command on oaths, the rabbis set up a double standard of credibility. Since they required a person to tell the truth when an oath was taken, then that person was free to lie if not under oath.

Contrary to what the law and the teachings of the rabbis permitted, Jesus banned all oaths. By doing this he abrogated the law concerning oaths. Instead of vows Jesus set forth the principle of absolute truthfulness. He denounced the evasions of the law on swearing which used heaven, earth, Jerusalem, or one's head as a substitute for God's name and indicated that all of these imply a reference to God. When a person says, "I swear," it is implied that God has been called down as a witness to his or her credibility. When a person is honest, all oaths are superfluous. The word of a truthful individual is more trustworthy than the word of a liar even though the liar should embellish it with the most solemn oath. Anyone who has a reputation for honesty does not need an oath to decorate his or her veracity.

Josephus,[4] the Jewish historian of the first century CE, tells us that the Jewish sect of Essenes was noted for fidelity, and what they said was firmer than an oath. He went on to say that they shunned oaths which they considered to be worse than perjury, and contended that if one could not be trusted to tell the truth without an oath that person was already condemned. The Essenes did permit an exception to their rule. When a candidate was admitted to the formal organization of the community, he had to commit himself to a binding oath.[5]

Today we might not find in Christian circles those who would swear by God to deep a vow or to tell the truth, but there are circumventions which are just as ridiculous. There are those who hoodwink the community into believing that they are telling the truth. They use such expressions as "God revealed to me to do this or that," "It is God's will that we embark on this venture," or "If I don't raise a certain amount of money, God is going to kill me." Some religious leaders think that they have received an authority from God through ordination, and this of itself is a validation of their integrity. God's name is degraded by these claims because the character of God becomes a mockery among believers.

Retaliation

The fifth antithetical saying of Jesus begins at verse 38. It is noticeable that a reference is not made to a commandment from the Decalogue. Rather Jesus goes back to the law or retaliation found in Exodus 21:22–25, Leviticus 24:19–21, and Deuteronomy 19:21. In all three of these passages the law of retaliation begins with "life for a life." Interestingly enough Jesus omits the "life for a life" phrase while including "eye for an eye and a tooth for a tooth." It is understandable that the phrase was omitted by Jesus because capital punishment was a matter for the courts to adjudicate. He was only interested in injuries which could be settled among individuals in their personal relationships.

Limited retaliation was a tremendous improvement over bedouin blood revenge in primitive society. Under retaliation the injured person was restricted in the amount of punishment that could be inflicted. The punishment could not exceed the amount received. In Jesus' day the Pharisees had already rejected the law of retaliation. The measure for measure rule did not apply. If personal injuries were committed, the injured party claimed reparations instead of injury in kind to the offender. The compensation included damages for pain, medical treatment, and loss of time from work. The Sadducees retained the law of retaliation.

Like the Pharisees, Jesus abrogated the tit for tat rule, but he went beyond the teachings of the Pharisees by ruling out reparations for injuries received. He set forth an attitude which was more in keeping with proper relations to others. He presented five examples to show the disciples how they were to respond when wronged. All of the actions proposed by Jesus were positive in nature and not negative.

(1) If someone strikes you on the right cheek, turn to him the other also. To hit a person on the right cheek was not a harmful blow physically. How can a man punch another on the right cheek unless he is left-handed? The backhanded slap on the right cheek was a form of insult. In rabbinic writings we learn that an insulting slap on the face deserved more compensation than a slap with intent to do physical harm. For physical injury an aggressor had to pay 200 zuz, yet for a backhanded slap and other forms of insult a man was required to pay 400 zuz.

Turning the other cheek is not passive resistance but aggressive love. Jesus insisted that we should not stand on our rights and claim reparations for wrongs committed against us. When we are insulted we are to show mercy rather than resort to litigation. Jesus called for mercy not justice. The law of equity cannot reconcile damaged relationships among people. It only enhances the estrangement between persons. We have to concern ourselves with the attitudes and dispositions of those who insult us. This requires more than measure for measure or saving face. It calls for Christian love, mercy, and compassion.

(2) What if someone wants to sue you? The second illustration is a case before civil court. Someone enters a suit against a person and gets a tunic in settlement. Jesus said that under these conditions the person sued should give his cloak as well. Under Jewish law the cloak of an individual was exempt from litigation because it served as a covering

and provided protection from cold weather. Jesus was saying that we should not stand on our legal rights but go beyond what the law requires.

(3) What if you were pressed into service? The third example is a reference to the Roman practice of impressing civilians into service for the government. The Persians instituted the system, and it was copied by the Romans. The situation assumed by Jesus is that of a Jew impressed into service as a baggage carrier for a Roman soldier of the army of occupation. If one of his disciples should be forced into service, Jesus said that he should double what was demanded. Instead of carrying the baggage one mile take it two miles. In this way he asserted his freedom by going above and beyond what the law demanded.

(4) What if someone begs you for something? This example as well as the fifth are the most difficult to understand. What traveler in the Middle East has not heard the cry *"Bakhsheesh"*? In that area of the world, begging is a way of life for many people. The same situation existed in Jesus' day. Some people made a profession of begging. To give to them encouraged deceit and idleness. To be sure, some were in desperate need of food and clothing, but begging as an institution downgrades a person. Possibly what Jesus meant was that a person not forced by law to give to a beggar could give as an act of mercy and love. We show our freedom by giving out of compassion rather then by compulsion.

(5) What if someone wants a loan? The last illustration is about a person who asks for a loan. The law could not force a person to grant a loan to a neighbor. Again Jesus was saying that we must exercise our freedom and give a loan out of compassion. We may not encounter situations today that correspond in detail to the illustrations given by Jesus. What we do see in the examples is the kind of attitude we should have in relating to others. We are not to stand on our rights and fight for strict justice, but we are to be merciful and overcome evil with good.

Love of Enemies

The last antithetical saying of Jesus in the Sermon on the Mount is, "You have heard that it was said, Love your neighbor and hate your enemy; but I tell you, Love your enemies and pray in behalf of those who persecute you." The command to love one's neighbor was well-known in Judaism, but "hate your enemy" did not occur anywhere in the Old Testament as a command. Some scholars suggest that the two clauses were joined together as a popular maxim in Judaism. Others believe that "hate your enemy" was inferred from the experiences of oppression by the Jews at the hands of their conquerors who hated God. Therefore, the Jews reasoned that those who hated God must be hated by God. If God hated his enemies, they were required to do the same.

The Jews stretched the command to love one's neighbor so that it could include the proselyte and resident alien in Palestine. But Jesus widened the circle of love to include enemies as well. He swept away all quibbling over distinctions between neighbors and enemies and commanded us to love all people. Love is not only a commitment of one's whole personality (thought, feeling, and will) to the best interests of another in spite of a hostile attitude toward us, but it also prompts us to pray in behalf of those who oppress us. We are to use our highest means of communication with God for the benefit of those who would do us harm.

Jesus gave three reasons why we should love our enemies and pray for those who persecute us. The first is that God's love is universal. He loves all people without any distinction (v. 45). Secondly, Jesus' disciples are to demonstrate a righteousness higher than that of the tax collectors and Gentiles, to say nothing of the Pharisees (v. 46–47). The third reason, but by no means the least, was that the disciples were to be like God in their love. They were summoned to reflect the character of God by refusing to discriminate in their love.

To be mature in an expression of love means to love as God loves.

The normal requirement for decent living is to love those who love us, but Jesus demanded that we love those who hate us. We are to be complete in our love as God is complete. Such a kind of love shows that we are indeed the children of God.

The Greeks had four words that meant love. Unfortunately in the English language we have only one word for love. We can love hot dogs, Chevrolets, apple pie, and people as well. We know that the word like should be used in place of love, but we take the popular expression whether it is right or not. The four Greek words for love were *eros, philia, storgē,* and *agapē. Eros* was generally used to describe sexual love or love for a adorable object, but sometimes it was employed to express friendship love. *Philia* was restricted to love for a friend. *Storgē* usually meant love of parents for their children, but frequently conveyed the meaning of patriotic love—the love for one's fatherland. *Agapē* was a colorless word that was seldom used. However, it was this word for love that the early Christians accepted to express God's relationship to us, our relationship to God, and our relationship to others. *Agapē* is the word selected in verses 43–46 as well as other sections of the New Testament to summon us to seek the best interests of others. The apostle Paul vividly expresses the characteristics of *agapē* in I Corinthians 13.

Notes

[1] *Mekhilta* on Exodus 14;2.

[2] C. G. Montefiore, *Rabbinic Literature and Gospel Teachings* (London: Macmillan & Co., 1930) 38.

[3] *Mishnah Yoma* 8.9.

[4] Flavius Josephus, *Wars of the Jews,* 2.8.6.

[5] Dead Sea Scrolls, *Manual of Discipline* 5:8.

Chapter Seven

RELATIONS OF KINGDOM RIGHTEOUSNESS

Matthew 5:17–48

by J. Estill Jones

The Relation of Christ to the Law (5:17–19)

The Law is treated as a genuine revelation from God and is joined here with the prophets. No more is said in the Sermon about the prophets for there is hardly any conflict possible in the messages of Jesus and the prophets. Their message was fulfilled and they were vindicated in his coming. But what about the Law? It was subject to contemporary interpretation and application.

Jesus came to give a testation to the Law, to authenticate it. A papyrus example of the use of *pleroō* reminds us that it may mean "to carry out the provisions of a contract." By authenticating the Law and the prophets he declares them to be genuine revelation. The Law was given originally to fit the Israelites for worship. A law is a means of implementing a principle and is always subject to that principle. The principle involved with Israel was the covenant relationship— Exodus 19:3–8 is implemented in Exodus 20.

Nowhere in these verses—these following six antitheses—does Jesus say, "The Law says, but I say." Jesus is not taking issue with the Law as an application of the covenant principle. He is taking issue with contemporary righteousness as it applied to the Law. He might well say: "I certainly did not come to destroy the Law. You've already done a beautiful job at that. I came to authenticate the Law as an implementation of the Covenant Principle."

Jesus, by sanctioning better implementations of the principle, hardly counseled the violation of any—yet, where their practice violated the principle it was a different story. The Law will last: it is an expression of God's will for his people. You cannot toss it off easily. It is genuine revelation.

The Relation of Kingdom Righteousness to Contemporary Righteousness (5:20–48)

Kingdom righteousness exceeds contemporary righteousness. T. W. Manson reminds us that "a righteousness based on those first principles and not on mechanical obedience to precept and tradition is the condition of entry into the kingdom." This excess (quantitative) may be achieved by a route less devious than that of contemporary righteousness. This excess (qualitative) describes a different sort of righteousness—one having to do with character producing conduct rather than conduct producing reputation. You do not behave yourself into a relationship. You relate yourself into a behavior. This righteousness has reference to the actor and the result of kingdom righteousness on another is rarely mentioned in this section. The actor determines the ethical quality of the act and not its result on another.

The method of presentation is by five or six antitheses. Jesus contrasts Kingdom Righteousness and Contemporary

Righteousness which is based on rabbinical interpretations and applications of the Law. Jesus in each instance returns beyond the application and the Law to the Principle. This is represented in the chart below.

Contemporary Righteousness	Kingdom Righteousness
a. no murder	no anger
b. no adultery	no lustful thought
c. divorce on condition	no divorce
d. no false swearing	no swearing at all
e. eye for eye	no retaliation at all
f. love your neighbor	love your enemy

Kingdom Righteousness Is Expressed in the Proper Treatment of One's Brothers and Sisters (5:21–26).

Anger violates the principle. This is the beginning of murder. If you are angry enough to call another *"raka,"* even the Sanhedrin has a stake in your expression. It is the equivalent of "you" in "Go away, *you*." An Israelite invited to meal with a Gentile was served swine flesh. *"Raka,"* he said. The daughter of a king was commanded to serve her lazy husband. *"Raka,* I'm the daughter of a king," she said. "Empty, Blockhead." Such anger evokes divine judgment. The word *"more"* is an accusation of moral defect, and is more reproaching than *"raka."*

Anger prevents worship. A Jewish rule understood that the more important religious obligation took precedence over the lesser. Hence, reconciliation was more important than sacrifice. Reconciliation with your fellow is more important than your compliance with the demands of a ritual —even the offering of a sacrifice. Here is the way to worship. Be reconciled quickly.

Kingdom Righteousness Manifests Inner Purity (5:27–30)

The lustful look is the beginning of the adulterous act. Insofar as the actor is concerned, adultery has already been committed, for he has violated the principle of inner purity and marital commitment. This is so serious that the eye is better sacrificed than for the look to be experienced, the hand is better sacrificed than for it to offend. This is the background for the section on divorce.

Kingdom Righteousness Rigidly Limits Divorce (5:31–32)

The paragraph on sexual deviation (perverted desire) prepares logically for this section on divorce, though this seems to be Matthew's arrangement and Matthew's material. Matthew offers it here because Matthew strictly interprets the Jewish law and understands no cause for divorce except that of adultery.

Contemporary righteousness allowed many grounds for divorce: if she bore him no children, if she became a deaf-mute, if she would not work, if he would not support her, if he would not have relations with her. Some of them appear to give the woman the right of divorce, and she probably did not have that right in most Jewish circles. In some circles the man had only to stand in the door of the home and say "I divorce thee." That was it—Matthew (and Moses) insist that a bill of divorcement must be given. The rabbis played with this—as to the material on which the bill was written. If, for example, it should be written on a cow's horn and the horn was not attached, then she merely took the horn with the statement. If the horn was still attached to the cow, then the husband had to give her the cow, too.

Was there any genuine cause for divorce? No, there was only one—violation of the marriage vow in adultery! This item is taken up again in Matthew 19:3–12 and is interpreted a bit differently in Mark 10:2–12. The vows of personal commitment which undergird the marriage relationship may be violated by the wandering eye. The dissatisfaction thus expressed is a tragic confession of failure in a human relationship on the part of the kingdom subject. There is, to be sure, forgiveness for this failure—but things may never be quite the same again. A man's a man for a' that... A woman's a woman for a' that and a' that. Neither is to be despised as to become the plaything, the toy of an irresponsible other. The kingdom subject is not to despise another so as to take advantage of a physical or emotional weakness —nor is he or she to prostitute another to his or her own selfish desires.

Kingdom Righteousness Makes Oaths Unnecessary (5:33–37)

"You have heard that it was said . . . ." And it was said in Leviticus 19:12, Numbers 30:2, and Deuteronomy 23:21 —"Repay your oaths." And the rabbis played with this concept. Two sections of the Mishnah are devoted to distinctions such as Jesus hints at here. Such oaths were popular in Judaism and are in the East today. Basic to the expression was the attempt to swear by something which did not demand the truth: I"ll swear by heaven . . . I"ll swear by the earth . . . I"ll swear by my head.

There is no escape from the demand of truth. Any such oath is binding: there is nothing by which you can swear and not be guilty of irreverence. Augustine wrote: "The Lord teaches that there is nothing so worthless among the creatures of God, as that anyone should think that he may swear falsely by it." Yet the sanctity of the object does not sanctify your spirit of oath-keeping. Only your own character can sanctify your oath. It would be silly for an honest man always to swear that this or that is true.

Your word "yes" or "no" is enough, Kingdom subject. Any additional word is of evil. Schaff has written "There is no more striking proof of the existence of evil than the prevalence of the foolish, low, useless, habit of swearing."

Kingdom Righteousness Denies the Right of Retaliation (5:38–42)

"You have heard that it was said. . . ." And it was said in Leviticus 27:17–21, Exodus 21:23–25, and Deuteronomy 19:21—even steven, exact exchange, like for like!

—But I say. . . ." Do not *antistenai*. Do not match the evil man in action. Do not act like he acts. Do not retaliate. The context determines the meaning here. Do not swap out with the evil person! Here are some examples:

(1) Cases of personal violence: turn the other cheek.
(2) Cases of legal action: give him your coat also (though forbidden in Exodus 22:25f., Deuteronomy 24:12f.).
(3) Cases of authoritative compulsion: "go with him two."
(4) Cases of taking advantage of your good nature: "give to anyone who asks"; be imposed upon.

What did he say?

(1) He did not speak in terms of nonresistance.
(2) He did not speak in terms of passive resistance.
(3) He spoke in terms of Kingdom Righteousness—of non-retaliation.

Note the emphasis on attitude. This would preclude passive resistance. Note the emphasis on personal relationship. This would preclude nonresistance. He said: Do not stoop to the level of your oppressors and persecutors. Overwhelm them with love.

Righteousness is more effective than retaliation in personal relationships. Jesus demanded human kindness—even when your fellow is doing you an injustice. Though he has forgotten his duty to you, you must love him. Jesus recognized the futility of evil—two wrongs do not make a right. Retaliation does not ease the hurt of a kingdom subject. You cannot successfully oppose evil by using evil weapons. Jesus had confidence in the power of goodness—to use it is not a sign of weakness but of power. The power and will to resist must always be the measure of personhood and of life itself. And what Jesus demands is not nonresistance, but a different kind of resistance. Evil is not to be opposed with its own arms, but with good, for in this manner alone can it be fully overcome. Goodness is active resistance.

Jesus is interested in the effect on the kingdom subject. He is not at this point of worrying about the recipient—even in giving. Let the kingdom person be imposed upon when he knows he is being imposed upon. What effect will this have on the actor? Luke's parallel (12:57–59) suggests that the kingdom subject give in to the adversary quickly. Let him get away with it. Have the attitude of peace.

Kingdom Righteousness Manifests Love for Enemies (5:43–48)

The antithesis is law and limited love versus kingdom righteousness and limitless love. It is law and discriminating love vs. kingdom righteousness and non-discriminating love.

"Thou shalt hate thine enemy" is Matthew's explanation of the inevitable result of loving your neighbor only—not the law.

In this fashion you will be acting as genuine children of the father. Like him—"like father, like son"—this is the aim of it. If God did not give indiscriminately, there would be material, physical chaos; if you do not love indiscriminately, there will be spiritual chaos. This is kingdom character, not good economics, social behavior or politics.

In this habit, this character, of indiscriminateness, you achieve "love unlimited." This is God's plan for you. When you achieve God's plan for you, you will be "perfect." You may have a spot or blemish, but you will have ripened (matured) to the point of God's plan. This is the kind of perfect in this regard, you will be a child of the father.

Augustine well said, "Love, and do as you please."

Chapter Eight

A Place for the Bull

Psalm 119:89-96; Matthew 5:17-20,48

by Linda E. Jordan

When Andrew Wyeth painted his picture called "Young Bull," someone had to stand and hold a ring in the animal's nose in order to keep it still long enough for Wyeth to get the critically fine details that characterized all his paintings.

After a while, the bull became so tame that he would follow Wyeth around the pasture and stand beside him while he painted. One day, in a gesture of affection, the bull nuzzled Wyeth's arm, causing a streak of paint across the canvas. According to the man who owned the farm (and the bull, too, I think), Wyeth decided to let the streak stand as a part of the painting.

Can you imagine the significance of that decision on the part of a perfectionist like Andrew Wyeth? If you are familiar with his other works, like "Christina's World," you know him to be a meticulous and consummate artist. And yet, amid his excellence, his control, his exquisite talent, and his deep commitment to precision, Andrew Wyeth made a place for the bull.

When I read this story in an American Baptist publication, it unsettled me. For as long as I can recall, I have been marked by compulsive behavior—striving to do everything right, to be perfect, to leave no room for error or failure. I grew up attending to the least points, the dots and the iotas of life. At least a part of me believed I could be perfect just as God in heaven is perfect.

David Burns, Director of Pennsylvania University's Institute for Cognitive and Behavioral Therapy, points out that our culture encourages two forms of perfectionism. One is achievement perfection—that is, being the smartest, the prettiest, Number One, earning our self-esteem by success. The other is romantic perfectionism—that is, expecting perfect relationships without conflict or failure, being critical of ourselves and others when flaws become inevitable.

Burns goes on to point out that what makes perfectionists miserable is not their high aspirations. To strive for excellence is healthy. It is the fear of disapproval, the fear of being unloved, the fear of being worthless when we fall short, that yield unhappiness.

Andrew Wyeth's story forced me to go back and examine a text that has long haunted me: "You must be perfect, as your heavenly Father is perfect."

God is limitless. God does not have to settle for chance or for error. God could insist, by definition, on the picture proceeding exactly as God wants it. God has both the skill and the power to ensure perfection. God's ideals and standards are never compromised, discarded, or minimized. And yet God allows us a part in the painting. God chooses for our imperfect contributions to stand in the eternal picture. And God uses our humanness to communicate the kingdom of God.

The Greek translated in Matthew 5, "Be ye perfect," is rendered more accurately, "Be mature, be complete, be sound." It connotes faithfulness more than flawlessness. It means to strive for goodness, not unqualified success. To be mature, to be complete, to be faithful is a part of God's nature we can imitate.

A friend of mine who grew up in Africa gave me a wonderful paradigm by which to understand this kind of

Godly perfection. He said the villagers gather and sit in a circle under a tree, and they ponder together a particular truth. The circle is said to be complete when everyone has contributed a word or point of view. The most significant aspect of their shade tree parliament, however, is that they always leave a space in the circle. The space represents room for surprise and mystery. It also reminds them that all human judgments are tenuous and therefore open to further insight. Only in the western world is the circle closed.

Our maturity and faithfulness are always contingent on keeping a space for growth and mystery, always making room for the bull, always recognizing that completeness does not mean closed-mindedness. Andrew Wyeth was being faithful, not careless, when he intentionally included the uncalculated brush stroke. By doing so, he did fulfill the essence and object of his painting—the young bull. In that respect, his painting was indeed perfect.

Truly comprehending the meaning of this text drastically alters the way we live. For one thing, we can begin to love and accept the bull within us. We can begin to recognize that our mistakes, our failures, and our imperfections do not have to undo us. In fact, they can contribute to our maturity, our sense of well-being, our excellence, our goodness. Carlyle Marney once said that to know that God loves us, warts and all, is what we all need in order to be whole.

Further, since Christian perfection is faithfulness and not flawlessness, we can stop clamoring for recognition and jockeying for position and dare to ask and discover, seek and find, listen and learn, fail, grow, and mature.

This means that:

—Adults will be willing to learn from children.

—Teachers will listen to their students.

—The moneyed will be informed by the experience of the poor.

—The educated will discover the truths of the so-called uneducated.

—The first world will be reshaped by the understanding of the third world.

Jesus challenged the perfectionists of his day, the Pharisees, to exceed their legalistic rightness and move more toward spiritual faithfulness. God's law was always intended to be a gift of life, not a burden and a barrier. God's law was always intended to be a gateway to human development and joy, not an instrument of judgment and guilt. St. Paul gives the image of a runner who strives, not to win, but to do his or her best. How easily and often we distort God's goodness and wholeness-giving.

For some reason that defies logic and explains grace, Andrew Wyeth made a place for the bull. By his act of openness, he did not diminish his talent, he enhanced it. And he taught me something critical about God's incredible perfection. God, in full maturity of love and goodness, allows us to be part of the picture. It is not an accident; it is an active choice.

Let us be faithful stewards of that mystery. Within us and in all that we do, O God, let us make a place for the bull. Amen.

Chapter Nine

War Prayer

Matthew 5:38–48

by *Thomas H. Graves*

The War Prayer by Mark Twain is one of the most incisive and pointed interpretations possible of Jesus' teaching to love one's enemies. Twain himself recognized the volatile nature of his poem when he refused to print it during his lifetime. He told a friend who pled with him to publish *The War Prayer*, "No, I have told the whole truth in that, and only dead men can tell the truth in this world. It can be published after I am dead." [1]

In Twain's story a congregation meets for prayer a day before the town's young troops march off to war. The service is centered on patriotic fervor and passionate prayer that God would protect their soldiers, bring them victory, crush the foe, and grant to their country untarnished victory. An aged stranger entered the church and moved to the front. Asking the minister to step aside, the stranger announced that he came from God's throne bearing a message: God will grant your prayer if you understand fully what it is you ask. Your prayer for victory is two prayers, said the stranger. You have given voice to one prayer, but there is an unspoken prayer for your enemy's annihilation and you must listen to it as well. Then the stranger stated the words of the congregation's silent prayer:

> . . . help us to tear their soldiers to bloody shreds with
>   our shells;
> help us to cover their smiling fields with the pale form of
>   their patriot dead;
> help us to drown the thunder of the guns with the
> shrieks of their wounded writhing in pain; . . .
> blast their hopes,
> blight their lives, . . .
> stain the white snow with the blood of their wounded
>   feet!
> We ask it in the spirit of love. . . . [2]

"That is also your prayer," said the stranger, "and if that is still an expression of your true faith, then speak," he said. When they did speak, the worshipers said that the strange man must be a lunatic for he made no sense, no sense at all.

A person must be a lunatic to talk of love of enemies. It is simply not possible. One must be crazy to expect persons to be perfect as God is perfect. It is not possible. In these verses we confront the point of greatest tension between the ethics of Christ and the practicality of human life. Is the Christian message simply an ethic for lunatics? Or is it the only way to live faithfully in the midst of a crazed society?

This passage begins with a reference to the ancient law of "an eye for an eye." One of the oldest law codes of human history, the Code of Hammurabi which dates from about 19 centuries before the time of Christ, defines clearly the laws of retaliation or *lex talionis*. This law placed restrictions upon revenge by insisting that one could not inflict more damage than one had suffered. The Old Testament law codes reflect such a view on several occasions, teaching a sense of fair revenge.

Jesus, in verses 39–41, recognizes the law of retaliation but goes on to say, "Do not retaliate in anger." He then gives three examples of non-retaliation. First, he speaks of being insulted with a slap across the cheek by the backhand of another. This would have been not so much an assault on one's body, as an attack on one's pride. Be ready to take more abusive insults we are taught.

Second, Jesus argues that we should abandon even our legal protection when responding to those who literally sue the pants off of us. In first century Palestine it was common to wear two garments, one a snug coat with sleeves, the other a looser outer cloak. The law offered personal protection by insisting that no one could be forced to give up both garments. But now Jesus taught that we are to offer both coat and cloak, even though our enemy would never expect such a generous response.

Third, is the common event of being forced to work for the soldiers of the occupying army. If forced to carry a soldier's gear for one mile, offer to carry it even further, says Jesus.

In every case we are encouraged to go beyond custom and law. When you are insulted and have the right to take offense, don't respond in anger. When you unfairly lose a legal case and have the right to keep some of your possessions, be ready to part with them as well. When you are forced into service by a soldier and have the right to limit what you will do, be ready to do even more. God's kingdom turns our modern system of individual rights and personal revenge upside down. This is revolutionary particularly in our American society so focused on the protection of individual rights. Is this the ethic for a lunatic?

In verse 42 Jesus offers a simple summary teaching: share. In so doing Jesus attacks another foundation of our modern culture, the stalwart protection of private property. It is again a revolutionary concept to suggest that as stewards of God's wealth we do not even own ourselves, that the disposition of our property should take into account at all times the needs of others.

In verses 43 and 44 Jesus refers to the foundations of Old Testament law by quoting, "Love your neighbor as yourself."

But once again Jesus introduces the revolutionary word, "Love your enemies," as if "neighbor" meant everybody. In his own ministry, Jesus demonstrated that "neighbor" means the Samaritan, the leper, the tax collector, the prostitute, and the sick. At the cross we see that neighbor even means the one who is killing you. For even then the words of forgiveness are spoken to the Roman soldiers.

With verse 48 the passage reaches its demanding climax: "Be perfect as your heavenly father is perfect." Surely the moral instruction has gone too far. Surely now it is in the realm of lunacy. Many try to deny the import of the message by the development of common dodges: it is hyperbolic speech that we don't need to take seriously; the purpose is to realize the impossibility of the task so we will throw ourselves on the mercy of God; it is meant for only the select few among us; it is not for this world but the world to come.

If Jesus meant these words, we are called to live by the teaching: be perfect and love your enemy. What would that mean? The word "perfect" does not refer so much to moral flawlessness as it does to being complete or full grown in our love of others. The word is used elsewhere in the New Testament to describe mature faith as seen in the unity of the church (Eph 4:13) and as demonstrated in the consistency of one's devotion and lifestyle (Jas 1:4). We are taught to love in all we do rather than to divide the world into persons we love and persons we hate.

The core of Jesus' instruction is seen in the admonition not to have a double standard. The flaw of revenge is that our actions are determined by others rather than by our relationship to God. Our actions must be determined not by our foes but by our God. When we act in hatred toward others who have mistreated us, we are giving control of our lives over to them. Repeatedly in the New Testament God is described as being "without partiality" (Acts 10:34; Rom 2:11; Gal 2:6; Eph 6:9). In this passage we are called to live with the same impartiality.

How is such an impartial lifestyle possible? We are given three clues in this passage. First, it is possible only insofar as we permit our actions to be determined by our relationship to God. The relationship with the divine is grounded in a sense of profound humility when we recognize that only by the grace of heaven's impartial mercy have we experienced God's love for us. Having acted as an enemy to God, yet having been undeservedly loved by God, how can we demand of others to be "worthy" of our love before it is offered?

Second, it is possible only if we actually give up ownership of our being to the loving care of God. In a society that worships care for self and the rights of oneself, these are perhaps the words of a lunatic. But in the kingdom of God there are values more important than self-protection. The issue is not one of legal rights but of love's consistent expression.

Third, there is one other base for establishing a lifestyle of loving one's enemies: the world's survival. Martin Luther King, Jr. rightly reminded us that in our modern world it is no longer a choice between violence and non-violence. It is a choice many times between non-violence and non-existence. We must learn to live with impartial love for the sake of the world's preservation.

A true story is told of a Latin American country during a time of revolution. An army officer arrested and tortured many of the persons involved in the insurrection. Revolutionaries were killed and treated in terribly brutal ways while in prison. In the end the revolution was successful and the former army officer found himself imprisoned with some of the former inmates now in charge of the government. A representative of the new government, who had himself undergone torture at the officer's own hand, came to the prison cell and found the officer expecting the revenge of torture and execution. "Go ahead and get it over with," the former officer cried. "No, you don't understand," said the new government official. "There's been a revolution and the days of hatred are over."

We have had a history filled with revolutions of the barricades. Now perhaps the time has come when we have the opportunity to proclaim a revolution of the heart. Never has a society so needed to hear the words of the "lunatic" on the cross: "Love one another, as you have been loved."

Notes

[1]Albert Bigelow Paine, *Mark Twain, A Biography*, (New York: Harper and Brothers, 1912) 1234.

[2]Mark Twain, *The War Prayer*, (New York: Harper and Row, 1971).

Chapter Ten

The Perils of Piety

Matthew 6:1-6,16-18

by Scott Nash

"Double-speak" is a common, though unappreciated, phenomenon. We find it, perhaps, most apparent and abundant in politics. Candidates use "double-speak" to avoid getting pinned down on prickly issues by taking a stand sufficiently indefinite to allow them to disclaim what others say they said. Or, they will appear to favor both sides of what is clearly an irreconcilable matter. When we recognize that "double-speak" is occurring, we are usually disappointed and accuse the person of "speaking out of both sides of the mouth."

To our dismay, Jesus appears to have been engaging in his own brand of "double-speak" in the Sermon on the Mount. In one part of the sermon he said, "You are the light of the world. . . . Let your light shine in such a way that people will see your good works and give glory to your Father who is in heaven."

The point he seemed to be making to those who were listening to him and trying to decide about following him was that, like light, they were to be visible in the world, shining forth for everyone to see.

Why would Jesus need to say this? Was it because he knew that many would-be followers have a tendency to be invisible in the world? Was it because he knew that some *do* take whatever light they have and hide it under a bushel basket? Was it because he knew that some who claim to be followers forget their reason for following, that they live so inconspicuously in the world that nothing in their lives ever directs anyone's attention to God?

It is true, isn't it, that Christians can become rather invisible in the world. In fact, there may be times when all of us would prefer anonymity over recognition. We certainly do not want to be accused of being "pushy" with our faith, and for good reason. Too many have discredited the Light by trying to force their Christianity on others—by the sword, by the vote, or by intimidation. Old style, collar-grabbing, door-knocking evangelism turns many of us off. It appears to be more noble, and certainly less offensive, to express our faith in quieter, less confrontational ways. Maybe it is even best to keep it to ourselves entirely. After all, our relationship with God, and everyone else's, is a personal matter.

Maybe we take the internalization of our faith even further. Maybe we understand our Christianity largely, or exclusively, in terms of how a person feels on the inside. Intensity of personal devotion is the key. Knowing that day by day our "love affair" with Jesus gets sweeter and sweeter is all we could ask for. "Me and Jesus Got a Good Thing Going," could be our theme song. The fire of intimacy with God burns deep within, but, alas, no light appears on the outside. We are *in*-spired, but not to do anything beyond our inner selves. In a sense our faith, as intense as it may be, is quite invisible.

No wonder Jesus said "Let your light shine!" Invisible Christianity lacks something crucial.

But then he came back just a little later in the same sermon and said, "Beware of practicing your piety before people in order to be seen by them." He said that when you give alms, you should do it quietly without fanfare. He said that when you pray, you should do it in the most private way imaginable. He said that you should fast without letting anyone know you are fasting. Practice your piety in private, he was stressing. Certainly these injunctions clash with his command to "shine!"

How do we account for what appears to be an incongruity here? Is Matthew the culprit, pulling various sayings out of their original contexts and rearranging them here in this sermon in such a way that they give an inconsistent message? Perhaps. Was Jesus himself somewhat inconsistent, emphasizing one point in an extreme way on one occasion and giving equally extreme emphasis to a counter point on another, as preachers have been known to do?

Obviously there is tension here between these sayings. The kind of tension encountered here, though, is not rare among the words of Jesus. In fact, all of discipleship seems to involve a certain tension. It's as if Jesus deliberately keeps his disciples on their toes, never allowing them (us) to settle down too comfortably. What else should we expect from the one whom we confess to be fully God and fully human?—a mouthful of tension no matter how we try to explain it!

"Double-speak" it may appear, but this is our word from the Lord, and this two-pronged word gives a clear warning about the dangers of practicing our piety. We are to practice our piety, that is to express our faith and do "religious" things, but we are to be aware of the pitfalls that threaten all our pious acts.

Perils abound when we seek to impress God with our piety.
Religious acts can be seen as a means of winning God's favor. In fact, most outward expressions of religion (sacrifices, prayers, songs, even almsgiving) seem to have their origins in a desire to please or appease some deity whose good will is considered a good thing to have. The mixture of motives that naturally arises within us as we approach God is the source of the tension and the peril of expressing our faith in tangible ways. Which of us does not want to be on God's good side?

Jesus once told a parable about two men who went into the temple to pray (Luke 18:9-14). One stood near the front and thanked the Lord that he was not the same as other people, especially not like the publican who stood in the back. He reminded God of his fervent prayers and his generous tithes. He was flaunting his piety in a way that he hoped would earn the favor of God. In contrast, the publican in the rear asked for mercy. Jesus asserted that the sinful publican rather than the pious Pharisee returned home justified. Jesus added a stern warning against all those who exalt themselves—"They will be humbled." He made it clear that God is not impressed by our religious acts.

And yet we continue the ancient scheme of trying to win God's favor by our pious deeds. In the Middle Ages the exercise of piety became institutionalized with the church's sanction. By performing prescribed acts of penance, one could gain forgiveness for sins. While the concept of penance was a healthy one in that it urged people to take sin seriously and not to take forgiveness lightly, it ran the danger of corruption and exploitation common to all religious acts. The system of institutionalized penance degenerated into a "junk bond" scandal wherein forgiveness for past and future sins could be secured through the performance of certain signs of piety, along with the payment of the proper fees, of course. Relationship with God was transformed into a business contract.

The system has changed, but the desire to win God's favor through demonstrations of our goodness has not left us. We sometimes still find ourselves making business arrangements with God. We may not make pilgrimages, recite prayer after prayer, or fast with gaunt faces, but we have our ways.

A young boy of eleven asked the pastor of a church if he could talk with him after the morning service. They met in the pastor's study, and when the pastor gently asked him what he wanted to talk about, an avalanche of tears exploded downward from the boy's eyes for several minutes. Finally, after considerable crying and stuttering, he was able to explain to the pastor that he felt he had not been a very good person. He had not been as nice to his mother as he should, and often he was not regular in his church attendance. He had also been in a scuffle that week with one of his friends at school. He wanted to know if there was something he could do to make it all up to God. He said he would be glad to help the pastor around the church. He would do whatever needed doing; he would even preach if the pastor would let him. He just wanted God to like him again.

Somewhere the boy had picked up a perspective that is shared by many—that if we do the right things, we can convince God to like us. Perhaps it is childhood conditioning that leaves us with the understanding that acceptance, affirmation, and a sense of self-worth are to be won by proving ourselves good enough to receive them. Certainly it is a childish way to approach God.

Jesus made it clear that God sees beyond the outward form of our expressions of piety into the inner realm of motivation. God sees past the act to the reason for our action, which Jesus asserted was far more important. If our reason for performing pious deeds is to impress God, God is not impressed.

Another peril awaits us whenever we would seek to impress others by our piety. Religious acts easily lend themselves to becoming the means by which we seek to earn another person's respect.

Perhaps the classic, and probably caricatured, example of this is the Pharisee. Even though there is good reason to believe that Pharisaic Jews were more authentic in their approach to God than a superficial reading of the Gospels suggests, it is easy to see why the Pharisee has become a scapegoat for much of our criticism of inauthentic faith. The portrait of the Pharisee we see in the Gospels, especially in Matthew, is that of an ostentatious, superficial, and self-serving person looking to his own righteousness rather than trusting in the grace of God. Undoubtedly some Pharisees resembled this picture, just as there have been many Christians who fit the mold. The extreme presentation of the Pharisees in the Gospels probably reflects not only the animosity of the early church's conflict with the synagogue, but also an awareness of the tendency toward self-righteousness that exists for Christians. Jesus' verdict on such action points to a basic defect in motive. He called such persons "hypocrites" and said that they did what they did in order to be seen by other people.

We may know better than to try to impress God with our piety. Still, we may feel and succumb to the temptation to impress others. Religion can often become the avenue for securing the kind of recognition that one has learned to expect in every dimension of life. Or, religion may provide a way to gain prestige for those who are excluded from other opportunities for achieving recognition and respect. To be "well thought of" may appear to some to be as important, if not more so, as to be on God's "good side."

One family in a small church made a large donation to that church every Christmas. It was their "Christmas present to the Lord." One year they bought all new pulpit furniture. Another year they presented the church with a new communion service. Another year they made a major contribution to the steeple fund, and the next year they gave generously to the organ fund. Always the gift would be in the name of some deceased member of the family. When possible, a plaque would be placed somewhere in the church to commemorate the gift. The other church members were always grateful and duly impressed with the family's generosity. What only a few members of the congregation knew, however, was that the members of the generous family never gave at any other time during the year. They essentially saved up all their tithes so that they could make one large and noticeable gift each year.

Some people are willing to give of their resources, time, and energy in great abundance, even sacrificially, but only if they are assured of receiving the appropriate recognition for their service. Some are willing to work hard and long hours for the Lord, but only if they can be in a position of leadership and prominence. The "behind-the-scenes "work is left for others. The question of motivation naturally arises. Why do they do what they do? Is it for love of God or for the praise of others? Can we be sure what *our* motives are?

Piety performed for praise earns its limited reward. Jesus said that the hypocrites had already received the reward they wanted, but it was a limited one. The language suggests that they were "paid in full." They wanted to impress others; they were successful. They would receive nothing more.

The implied warning in Jesus' harsh words is that we examine our own hearts as best we can to discern our real motivation for pious deeds. Is our objective to shine so that others may see God in a better light, or do we seek to relish the glow of the spotlight on ourselves?

Perhaps the most insidious peril, however, is that we would seek to impress ourselves by our piety. Perhaps it is this peril that underlies the desire to impress God and others. We want to feel good about ourselves.

Religious acts may be seen as a means for confirming our own self-righteousness. Again, the Pharisee becomes our scapegoat here, allowing us to project all of our own inclinations toward self-service onto a figure who is more victim than villain. In so doing we reveal much more about the self-serving strain that haunts our own religious experience than we do about any spiritual deficiencies of first century Judaism. Whenever we congratulate ourselves that we are better than that, when we thank God that "we are not like that Pharisee," we are actually betraying how much we, ourselves, embody the great threat to genuine piety symbolized in the characterization of the Pharisee. To pit ourselves against the "Pharisee" makes us feel better. We have our reward.

Religious faith is one dimension of life where the meeting of personal needs is a primary matter, and a primary personal need is self-esteem. Much, if not all, of our expressions of piety, our performance of good deeds, is connected to our efforts to satisfy certain inward needs. Even our most altruistic acts are not empty of some self-satisfaction. It makes us feel good about ourselves to help others. We learned this early on, maybe the first time we consciously felt that warm sensation of being told how "good" we were because we shared our toys. So deeply entrenched is our need to feel good about ourselves that it inevitably colors our reasoning and shapes our behavior, even in our relationship with God.

The peril we face is that of allowing the satisfaction of deep, personal needs to dictate our religious actions. We may recognize that we have such needs. We may also recognize doing "good things" brings a certain satisfaction to many of these needs. It does make us feel better about ourselves. But this is far different from allowing the quest for need-satisfaction to become the driving force in our expressions of piety.

Piety stemming from self-centered motives misses the mark of genuine discipleship. True discipleship involves responding to the invitation to let your light shine so that God is seen in a glorious way. As difficult as it proves to be, we are called to do good things which make us feel good, not because they make us feel good but because they are the right things to do, and in doing them we reflect the light of God.

Jesus said, "Let your light shine . . . but be careful!" We are called to be visible in the world, but never for the sake of being seen. The tension remains for disciples who would follow this two-pronged command. Knowing when and how to shine and when and how to stay in the shadows is not easy. Those who would be genuinely pious must be constantly alert to the perils of trying to be impressive in their piety.

Chapter Eleven

Prayer and the Kingdom

Matthew 6:7–15

by J. Mark Lawson

In the midst of his exhortations concerning the exercise of faith, Jesus gives special attention to the act of prayer. Jesus regarded prayer as an intensely personal moment of communion with God to be approached with great care and reverence. He even seemed to discourage public prayer except as it served to express a corporate communion with God that was already taking place. In verses 7–15 Jesus digresses long enough to give very specific instruction about how to pray, even to the point of offering a model prayer.

A False Test

"And in praying, do not heap up empty phrases as the gentiles do, for they think they will be heard for their many words."

There seems to be a long-standing myth in Christian tradition that the length of a prayer is a measure of the piety of the one who is praying. The longer a prayer is, the more "spiritual" the one praying appears. In this verse, however, Jesus says quite bluntly that no relationship exists between the length of a prayer and its merit. In the following verse, he pokes fun at those who offer lengthy prayers.

"Do not be like them, for your father knows what you need before you ask him."

Unnecessarily long prayers can be of no benefit to God. Long, repetitive prayers sound as if God is receiving information about us that God did not already have; as if the likelihood of their being answered is increased if we keep saying the same things over and over. But God knows our needs before we pray. The benefit of prayer is not the information we pass on to God, but rather the strength we receive from approaching God.

That does not mean that God does not in any way benefit from our prayers. The Bible clearly witnesses that God is affected by our prayers. Abraham's prayer for Sodom and Moses' prayer for the Israelites had profound impacts upon God. Jesus' understanding of prayer as a moment of intimacy with God implies that God is as much a party to the moment of prayer as we are. But the benefit God receives from prayer is more in our willingness to be in fellowship with God than in the content of what we say.

A Model for Prayer

In verses 9–13 Jesus offers a model prayer that sums up the quality of our relationship to God as well as the kinds of intercession that reflect true faithfulness. A quick glance at the prayer reveals two things about its construction. First, it is quite brief. No words are wasted. Second, it falls into two roughly equal parts. The first half is about God's glory, the second half about our own needs.

"Pray then like this: 'Our Father who art in heaven . . .'"

At the very outset, the prayer confesses the paradox of the Christian understanding of God's nature. We believe that the God who created heaven and earth is also intimately concerned for each one of us. In the same breath we confess the transcendence and the immanence of God. God is over all, yet in all. God rules over the whole universe, yet is able to number the hairs on own heads.

". . . hallowed be thy name."

The Greek word translated "hallowed" has been the subject of much discussion among scholars. On the surface it simply means "holy" or "sanctified." But that God's name is holy is more than obvious. There is yet a deeper meaning to the word "hallowed" as Jesus uses it here.

The act of naming was given great significance in the ancient world. To name something meant to claim control over it. God gave Adam the privilege of naming the animals (Gen 2:19–20) as a sign of the dominion humanity was given over them. Because naming implies control, and at worst manipulation, God was never named. When Moses was confronted by God in the burning bush, he asked the Lord to reveal his name so that he could identify God to Pharaoh. God's response was an ambiguous form of the Hebrew verb *hayah* ("to be"), which might be translated in any tense: "I was who I was; I am who I am; I will be who I will be." In effect, God's "name," *YHWH* (as it would be spelled if the Hebrew letters were written in English), is a non-name that insists God will not be subject to the manipulation of God's people and is therefore distinct from all other named gods in the ancient world. Consequently, the Jewish tradition to this day resists pronouncing *YHWH*. Whenever it appears in the text, orthodox Jews simply insert "The Lord" (*Adonai*) in order to avoid violating the sacredness of God's name.

When Jesus instructed his disciples to call upon God as Father, and more specifically as *Abba* (a term of endearment used by little children with their parents) he raised quite a stir. Conservative Jews surely saw Jesus treading into dangerous territory, encouraging an intimacy with God that had been prohibited by the law of Moses. Was not *Abba* a name that compromised the holiness of God? As one who understood the holiness of God more supremely than anyone, Jesus was well aware of the risk involved in calling upon a "Father" God. The counsel to acknowledge the name as "hallowed" is a reminder that the naming of God is very different from the naming of anyone else. God is not only holy, but also distinct. The name by which God is addressed in prayer is a name given by God's "Son." It is qualitatively different from any name that arises out of human experience. Our intimacy with God is effected by God's grace, not by our ability to manipulate or control God. We do not bring God down to our level; God stoops down to dwell with us in Christ.

> *"Thy kingdom come, thy will be done on earth as it is in heaven."*

The kingdom of God has already been inaugurated in the presence and ministry of Jesus, but it awaits its fulfillment. Jesus instructs us to be in constant prayer for the kingdom's fulfillment. How different would our prayers be if we took this instruction seriously? Do we regularly pray for the kingdom? Or is it our habit to jump immediately into the anxieties of the present age that we want resolved today? Jesus admonishes us to voice all our prayers in the context of an ultimate hope for God's kingdom. To preface our personal intercessions with this ultimate hope will place our wants and needs in their proper perspective.

But beyond praying for the coming of the kingdom, Jesus exhorts us to pray for an increasing openness to it in this present age. The fulfillment of the kingdom will require calamity, for the kingdom is at odds with the values of a world under the rule of sin and violence. To pray for the kingdom "on earth as in heaven" is to pray for that calamity to be diminished by the decisions of people on earth to forsake the kingdom of darkness and choose the kingdom of light. It is to pray that the kingdom will find residence in the hearts of people before it is fulfilled, so that the dismantling of the reign of sin will be accomplished to some extent even before sin is utterly defeated. The more people welcome the kingdom's coming in the present time, the less calamity will be necessary to destroy sin in the end time.

The next three petitions concern human need. And yet, all three are offered in the shadow of this ultimate concern for God's kingdom. All three have a double meaning, addressing both the present and the future.

"Give us this day our daily bread."

We ask for God to provide for our day-to-day physical needs. Since the body is integral to the whole spirit that makes up each one of us, we must have physical nourishment to accomplish the tasks of the kingdom. But this seemingly simple prayer has another more subtle meaning. The word translated "daily" (*epiousian*) is almost without parallel anywhere in the Greek language. This mysterious word, according to many scholars, seems to mean "tomorrow"—thus, "Give us our bread for tomorrow." But what would that mean?

Jesus may well have in mind the familiar Old Testament image of the banquet table, a symbol of the fulfilled kingdom. The table was a rich metaphor for the kingdom because it expressed the hunger of the present age for the justice and mercy of God unfettered by the world's sin. The Israelites hoped for that time when the presence of God would be as manifest as one seated at the head of the dinner table. God's people would feast together on God's love, grace, mercy, and justice in all their abundance. No more would the Israelites taste only morsels of that day in the midst of their struggles. In the kingdom justice and righteousness would roll down like the waters of an ever-flowing stream and be supplied as the abundance of an eternal harvest.

Jesus coined a term that would denote both our physical needs as well as the deepest need for the hope of the kingdom to be fulfilled. In one breath we ask for the bread to fill our stomachs and the bread of tomorrow—the feast of God's kingdom.

"Forgive us our debts, as we forgive our debtors."

This petition, too, is very practical. All of us struggle with forgiveness. How is it that we can put offenses committed against us in the past so that they do not create obstacles in our relationships? And yet, in praying this way, we remind ourselves that God's forgiveness of us depends on our willingness to forgive others. Jesus adds an editorial note in verses 14 and 15:

"For if you forgive men their trespasses, your heavenly Father also will forgive you. But if you do not forgive men their trespasses, neither will your Father forgive your trespasses."

Parishioners have often said to me with some frustration, "I don't know what you mean by the forgiveness of God. I've never experienced it." Whenever I hear a remark such as this, my immediate response is, "Is there anyone in your life whom you have been unable to forgive?" Almost always the answer is "Yes." "Then that's why you haven't experienced God's forgiveness," I will reply.

"But isn't God's forgiveness a free gift?" "Why does Jesus place this condition on forgiveness?" "Is it reasonable for God to expect us to forgive every offense committed against us, no matter how great?" Queries like these are real. They cut to the heart of the ethics of discipleship. Forgiveness is never easy. It is a process that sometimes takes years, depending on the seriousness of the offense committed. But it is important to note that Jesus' word for forgiveness has the root meaning "letting go." It may be that the most, and best, any of us can do is to release the anger we feel over the debts held against us. Forgiveness does not mean that the offender is no longer held accountable for his actions. It means that the one offended no longer takes responsibility for the accountability of the offender. The energy required to hold a grudge and remain personally committed to correcting a personal injustice is strong enough to impede our ability to receive anything from God. With every offense, no matter how great, there comes a time to let go of the anger and give it to God.

But this petition addresses more than the practicalities of forgiveness. The word "debts" is too conspicuous not to have a double meaning. It harks back to God's commandments in Leviticus relating to Sabbath. Specifically, it calls to mind the "Year of Jubilee" commanded in Leviticus 25. After seven periods of seven years, the people of Israel were to erase all debts and return all land to its original owners. In other words, Jubilee was a Sabbath for the Israelite economy that would correct all its excesses that had ensued in the last half century. As far as is known, the Year of Jubilee was never actually observed in Israelite history. There were too many creditors and too little good will to pull it off. Thus, the poor, whose land had been seized in hard times and had become tenants on their own property, became trapped in a usurial system and lost all hope of ever owning land. Had the Year of Jubilee been observed, the inequalities of the economy could have been corrected.

Since no one in human authority was willing to institute Jubilee, the poor came to associate it with the coming of a Messiah, believing that when God established the kingdom, their poverty would be addressed by a Messiah who would

forgive their debts. In Isaiah 61 the Year of Jubilee is associated with the Suffering Servant, who would later be identified
with Jesus. In fact, Jesus began his ministry in Nazareth by
reading this Isaiah text and proclaiming that his ministry
would fulfill the hope for Jubilee (Luke 4:16–21).

Thus, Jesus' model prayer calls upon us to pray for the
fulfillment of Jubilee: for all debts of every kind to be erased,
and for justice and equity to prevail. Jubilee has already been
inaugurated through Christ, in whom our debts against God
are erased. But Jubilee will not be complete until we in turn
erase the debts against us, and until societies of economic
inequities embrace God's justice. The kingdom will be a
realm without debt and poverty, for the kingdom is the
product of God's reconciling work in the world.

"Lead us not into temptation, but deliver us from evil."

All of us need the strength of faith when faced with
hardship. We need help from God in standing firm when our
faith is tested. This prayer does not imply that we are
tempted by God. An alternative translation would be, "Lead
us not into trial and hardship." Life's difficulties will find us
one way or another, especially if we are serious about
discipleship in a world of violence. We do not need for God
to create hardship for us. What we need is for God to deliver
us from the evil in the midst of hardship—the despair that
can crush our spirits and the terror that can paralyze our
faith.

At the same time, this petition concerns the coming of the
kingdom. Especially in the first Christian century, believers
understood that the closer the kingdom was to its fulfillment,
the more violent the world became. The persecution by the
Romans no doubt fed this conviction. It seemed that the
powers of darkness were mustering all their strength desperately to resist the coming of God's judgement upon them.
While contemporary Christians in America do not suffer as

they did, many of us still believe that more violence, not less, will precede Christ's return. The world is getting worse, not better, so that the most important time to stand firm is the most difficult time to remain faithful. And so John's Revelation assures persecuted Christians that the present sufferings are a prelude to the establishment of the New Jerusalem. Our prayers and our worship, though they seem unheard and unacknowledged in the days of the great beasts, are nonetheless of great effect in heaven, where the angels are prepared at God's commend to announce the coming of Christ, who will commence the final hour of history by destroying all evil in one swift, uneventful battle.

Thus Jesus instructs us to offer our personal day-to-day petitions in the larger context of our hope for the kingdom. Even the smallest of requests should fall from our lips in the shadow of our faithfulness to the kingdom.

The Church's Doxology

When Christians recite this prayer in public worship, they normally add a doxology that is not found in any early manuscript of the New Testament: "For thine is the kingdom, and the power, and the glory forever, amen." Since it is an addition to the original prayer, should we cease pronouncing it?

I do not think so. The doxology is as old as some New Testament writings, since it appeared in the *Didache*, a teaching manual published near the beginning of the second century. It does not make sense that we should not say these words only because Jesus did not say them. We freely quote Paul, Peter, and John. Why not the early church? This doxology is a piece of ancient Christian heritage that reflects not only the importance of Jesus' prayer from the earliest days of the faith, but also the early church's strong "Amen!" to all that Jesus was teaching through the prayer.

Two More Lessons

Now that we have examined the whole prayer, we can glean two additional lessons from it. First, it evidences no conflict between concern for daily needs and believing in the imminence of the kingdom. We should live like Jesus is coming tomorrow, but that does not mean we should quit living today. Such was the mistake of the Essenes that Jesus alluded to in 5:13–16. In preparing for the Messiah, they had withdrawn from ancient society in the interest of purity. In every generation, there have been millenialists who quit their jobs, sold their homes, or sat on the rooftops waiting on Jesus. But the imminence of the kingdom does not negate the importance of our daily struggles and needs. Jesus wants to find us ministering and living faithfully, not waiting passively, when he returns.

Another lesson in this prayer is that having our daily needs met depends upon rightly understanding our relationship to God. First, we must acknowledge who God is, then offer petitions. First, we give glory to God, then we seek to have our needs met. Until we understand our dependence upon God for all we are and have, we cannot expect God to give to us.

Chapter Twelve

Forgive and Forget

Matthew 6:12

by William E. Flippin

We have all heard the familiar quotation from Shakespeare: "To be or not to be, that is the question." Borrowing from Shakespeare, we can ponder: "To forgive or not to forgive, that is the question." This question of life, so easy to ask, produces no easy answers.

To forgive or not to forgive?—how one decides this dilemma is of eternal consequence. To forgive or not to forgive?—what we ultimately do in responding to this question may be the one difference in our attainment or loss of eternal life. Forgiveness, then, has the potential to send one to heaven or to hell.

Forgiveness is one of the easiest things to do. But on the other hand, forgiveness is one of the hardest things that a Christian must do. It is something that can be done with the mouth quite easily, but too often it never reaches the heart. Forgiveness can be the sincere desire of the heart, but at the same time it may never be done with the mind. We can say we have forgiven, and yet we may never forget.

To forgive is a simple thing to do, but at the same time, forgiveness is one of the most complex virtues that a Christian must master. But while forgiveness is easy, it is not to be taken lightly. Forgiveness is so vitally important that Jesus incorporated its meaning and philosophy into the prayer that he taught his disciples: "Forgive us our trespasses just as we forgive those who trespass against us."

The Living Bible says it this way: "Forgive us our sins just as we forgive those who have sinned against us." If we cannot and will not forgive others, God cannot and will not forgive us.

I have absolutely concluded that I need the Lord to forgive me.

I was born in sin and shaped in iniquity—I need the Lord to forgive me.

Sometimes I fall short of the Glory of God—I need the Lord to forgive me.

Sometimes I may say the wrong thing, or I may do the wrong thing, or I may go to the wrong places—I need the Lord to forgive me.

Sometimes the devil gets on my trail—I need the Lord to forgive me.

I'll think the wrong thing; I'll pray the wrong prayer—I need the Lord to forgive me.

I'll sing the wrong song; I'll walk the wrong walk; I'll talk the wrong talk—I need the Lord to forgive me.

And the word of God says that God wants to forgive us, no matter what we've done. But again, it is up to us: "To forgive—or not to forgive?"

We are reminded: "As we forgive ... God will forgive us." The question remains, since this thing called forgiveness is so important, Why can't we do it? What keeps the Christian from forgiveness? Why is it so hard for a child of God to forgive others, just as we desire God to forgive us?

The primary reason we cannot forgive others is a matter of pride. Isaiah 28:1 says, "Woe to the crown of pride." Proverbs 8:13 teaches that the Lord hates evil, hates arrogance, and hates pride.

We all know that when a spirit of pride is present, destruction soon follows. "Pride cometh before a fall."

Pride keeps us from forgiving one another. Self-righteous pride, arrogant pride, keeps us from forgiving the way we should. It is better sometimes to swallow our words and our pride, rather than to have to eat our words later. We have been deceived by being led to believe:

If we forgive, we will appear soft.

If we forgive, we will appear easy.

If we forgive, somebody might call us a fool and a push-over.

> If we forgive, we're afraid we will be taken advantage of again.

> If we forgive, than we feel justified when we say, "I'll forgive you, but don't let it happen again."

But the word to us is . . . when we learn how to forgive, we can be forgiven; when we learn how to forgive, we will be like Jesus.

So, every child of God ought to pray:

Lord help me to forgive.

Lord teach me how to forgive.

Lord show me how to forgive.

Lord guide me how to forgive.

I remember that one day as a child I asked someone how many times we had to forgive before we can could out fighting? Matthew 18:21 was quoted to me: "But I say unto you . . . 'Forgive seven times seventy!'" I saw then that there was a loop-hole. I could forgive 490 times and on the 491st time, I could fight back—I could get even! "No," my instructor said, "Jesus wants you to keep on forgiving . . . forgive until you don't have any more to give." In this life, we must learn to forgive and forget.

The story has often been told how one day a new governor discovered that one of his childhood friends was in the penitentiary. The friend had been there for over fifteen years. Upon discovering this, the governor decided to visit his friend. They spent hours reminiscing boyhood tales. When the governor returned to his office, he decided that he would give his prisoner-friend a pardon. He went back to the prison to visit his friend in a few weeks with the pardon in his pocket. Before he told the prisoner the good news, he thought he would ask: "If you could be a free man, what would be the first thing that you would do?" His friend, the prisoner of fifteen years, said, "The first thing that I would do is go to the judge and the accuser that put me here and kill them for what they did to me." With this, the governor sadly returned to his office, never offering freedom to his friend.

In this life we must learn to forgive and forget. For fifteen years, that man held hate in his heart. He would never see freedom because he had not learned to forgive and let things in the past stay in the past.

The best example of forgiveness is seen in Jesus on the cross of Calvary. Even in that horrible place, he found forgiveness to be the order of the day.

Before he took his final breath, he forgave.

Before he pulled off his mortal frame, he forgave.

Just before he stepped into the paradise of eternity, he forgave.

He negated his own pain, and he forgave—knowing that forgiveness was a pain-easer.

He negated his own imprisonment, and he forgave—knowing that forgiveness was not his imprisonment, but his flight to freedom.

He negated his own misery, and he forgave—knowing that forgiveness was not misery but was, indeed, the mercy of God.

He forgot about his personal agony, and just before the daylight of his life turned to the midnight of death . . . he forgave.

In this Christian life you may be required to forgive when you are at your lowest point. You may have to forgive when you are your weakest. You may have to forgive when you are the most hurt. In the church sometimes, you will have to forgive even though you know you are right. We cannot just forgive those folks we like. We cannot just forgive those folks who like us.

Don't fight back.

Don't hold a grudge.

Don't make yourself sick.

Don't act little as they do.

Please forgive and forget.

Be still, hold your peace, and let the Lord fight your battle.

Victory is yours when you remind yourself, "Forgive us our debts as we forgive our debtors." We must do this because . . .

He has vindicated us.

He had set us free.

He has released and pardoned us.

We have been excused and cleared.

We are liberated.

People can do anything against us, but we need not strike back. Rather we must say: "Father, forgive them." People can scandalize your name and speak all manner of evil against you. Please don't treat them as they treat you, but say, "Father, forgive them."

How can we do this? All forgiveness is motivated by love. You have to love everybody, if you want to see Jesus—if you'll ever learn to forgive.

Do you remember these words?

"For God so loved the world that he gave his Son" . . . to forgive.

"God commended his love toward us while we were sinners" . . . to forgive.

"He has loved us with an everlasting love" . . . to forgive us.

"I know the love of many shall wax cold; men shall turn to iniquity". . . but we need to turn and forgive.

"Father forgive them for they know not what they do."

"Love your enemies. Pray for them that despitefully use you."

Forgive? Forget? Let love lift you.

I was sinking deep in sin, far from the peaceful shore.
Very deeply stained within . . .
  wouldn't forgive,
  wouldn't turn to God,
  wouldn't love,
but the Master of the sea heard my despairing cry,
and from the waters . . . lifted me. Now safe am I.

Jesus keep me near the cross so that I may experience the fullness of your forgiveness . . . and forgive others. Amen.

Chapter Thirteen
The Riddle of Life
Matthew 6:25–33

by Carole Harvey Penfield

If you were to name the central riddle of your life, what would it be? The dictionary defines "riddle" as a question or a statement requiring thought to answer or understand. As you strive to live an authentic human life, what riddle, what puzzle are you seeking to solve or overcome or simply endure?

Near the end of the Lawrence and Meg Kasdan film *Grand Canyon*, one character says to another, "Part of your problem is that you haven't seen enough movies. All of life's riddles are answered in the movies."

Of course, it is not necessary to see movies to know about the riddles that life presents. All you have to do is get up in the morning and try to get along, or lie awake in the lonely silence of the night, or struggle to hold it together in the face of the fact that in this world things get broken—bodies and hearts and dreams.

Films that engage our imaginations do so because they reach into the depths of our riddles, probably not answering them but so poignantly reframing them that our angle of vision is shifted. One commentator said about the film *Grand Canyon* that it grabs you and takes you to your own life. R-rated though that film is, I therefore invite you into my reflections on it and its reflections on our world, which after all is not without its own obscenities, and to do that reflecting in dialogue with some words of Jesus Christ, who also knew about life's realities and riddles. This exercise is not to re-view a film but to take us to our own lives and shift our angle of vision on the riddles we find there.

The film's first words are these: "When are you going to realize that nothing can be controlled? It's the central issue in everyone's life . . . Look around you. Everyone is struggling for control. You know what it is they're trying to control? Fear. They're trying to control their fear." Thus begins a two hour, wide screen, living color depiction of contemporary nightmares, where you are abandoned and life insurance for children is peddled door to door in the ghetto, where relationships falter and lives are emptied of meaning. As another character put it later? "The world isn't supposed to work like this. Everything is supposed to be different than what it is."

Into this kind of world Jesus Christ has spoken: "Do not worry." Five times in this part of the Sermon on the Mount we hear him repeat the word for "worry," which literally has to do with being distracted, torn between how things are and how things might be. Worry is futile; it eats out our guts and undermines our motivation, to be sure, but in this world where everything is supposed to be different than what it is and the central issue of our lives so often is trying to control our logical and legitimate fear, how can we not worry?

Jesus was talking about life's basic necessities of food and clothing, which by extension may be understood as all that sustains and shelters life. What do we most fear losing? What essentials to our well-being are threatened by the wrongness of the way things are? Look them square in the face and name them.

We worry about disease and divorce and death. We worry about losing our jobs and our dreams and our loved ones and sometimes even our minds. We worry about violence within families and in cities and on the other side of the world. We worry about ethics in state government and economics in our nation and ecology around the globe. We even worry about our worries and feel guilty about them, hearing Jesus ask which of us by worrying can add a single hour to our span of life, knowing only too well the cruel fact that worry lessens quality and length of life.

If we look too long and too hard at what we fear, we are lost to our worries, distracted by and drawn toward the very thing we fear. My son, Matthew, called me at this exact point in my reflecting to ask what I was preaching about. When I said Jesus' words, "Do not worry," he told me what his experience as an eighteen year-old college freshman has taught him. "Worrying is something you do to yourself," he said. "Turn your head and change your perspective. You might see things a different way."

It is a matter of perspective. Stop being distracted and look the other way, says Jesus.

In one of the overlapping references to the film's title, one of *Grand Canyon*'s characters tells of a visit to the Grand Canyon. "You sit on the edge of that thing and you just have to realize what a joke we people are—a split second we've been here, the whole lot of us, each one of us a piece of time too small to get a name. The rocks are laughing at me, I can tell, me and my worries."

But Jesus said, "Look at the birds of the air, how God feeds them. Consider the lilies of the field, how God clothes them. Are you not of more value than they?"

In the awesome immensities and complexities of God's creation, it is true that we are small, tiny specks of flesh here only for a split second in the vast scale of infinity and eternity. Yet the One who creates and cares for all that is values us above the rest, and will that One not much more care for us?

Stop being distracted by the fear of what you might lose, Jesus is saying, and look square in the face of the final truth about your lives which can never be lost.

After a number of us from church had seen and discussed *Grand Canyon*, as I was driving two people home, one began to tell me how years ago he lost his faith in confusion over an apparent conflict between science and religion. What brought him back to seek the face and words of Jesus Christ was not a resolution of that conflict but a growing conviction that in the midst of all life's troubles we are not alone. "I know," he said, "that something cares."

Something cares. If we believe that we are lost and alone in the cosmos and it is all up to us to solve the riddles of life, we had better stay up nights worrying because the situation is hopeless. If we believe that all we have is blind fate or dumb luck to see us through, we may as well admit that we are not going to get very far.

But if there is something that cares, something we can count on, the God whose love Jesus Christ came to reveal and embody, we can expect whatever it takes to turn what is into what ought to be. We can expect angels and miracles and people of good will freed from their fears to turn toward hope and each other.

In the course of the film a couple separately experience angels and miracles, and together move toward a new perspective on life. Mack is saved from being crushed under a bus by a woman who reaches out, as he says, literally to yank him back from the edge; he is saved from gang violence by a tow truck driver. "Was she for real," he wonders, "or was she sent from somewhere?" Was she an angel? Without answers he is nevertheless impelled to reach out to yank others back from edges where life brings them. "I do these things and I wake up the next morning amazed," he muses.

After Claire finds an abandoned baby she tells Mack, "I believe there's a reason I found her . . . You can't go back and make it not happen, some kind of connection has been made that has to be played out . . . Maybe it's a miracle. Maybe we don't have experience of miracles and we're slow to recognize them."

And Jesus said, "Seek first the kingdom of God, and all these things will be yours as well."

"Seek" is the positive imperative parallel to the negative imperative, "Do not worry." It is second person plural in form, addressing to a community of people the truth that God's kingdom comes where God's will is being lived out communally, collectively, corporately, cooperatively by people whose perspectives have been transformed from worry to seeking. Angel visits are multiplied, miracles received are reciprocated, and a network of relationships flourish that weigh life's balance toward the good. The human response that perpetuates the cycle is as much a miracle as the event that precipitates it.

Who but God knows the line between objective happening and subjective experience, between miracle and mundane, and does it matter? Whether coincidence and serendipity and synchronicity, or in fact angels and miracles sent from the very hand of God, the connections that link our lives just might save us and all that we hold dear and the whole world from toppling over the edge into doom, if we can only see them sufficiently to participate. It will take a myriad of miracles to fix our world, but miracles do happen when we have eyes to see and let them be our focus instead of worry.

There are so many riddles we seek to solve with our lives. Lawrence Kadan articulates the central riddle of his film and his view of life this way: "The tension is always between two perspectives, that we're only here for a second and meaningless on the face of this big rock, and we have to live our lives as best we can and find some meaning in them."

God answers that same riddle through Jesus Christ both human and divine entering into space and time to grant us perspective: "Stop worrying; you are of more value than everything on this big rock that God created and cares for; start seeking to see what God is about and to be part of it; in that seeking you will find the deepest desires of your hearts fulfilled."

God continues to grant us meaning through a mysterious mixture of happenings and emissaries both natural and supernatural—the mystery of Christ alive in us and the whole world. Sometimes angels visit us and sometimes we are God's angels to one another. Often we cannot tell the difference and never does it matter. What matters is that we can so count on God that we can count on ourselves to be part of God's miracles.

The final line of *Grand Canyon* is spoken as the characters gather at the edge of the actual Grand Canyon to behold its immensity, and one of them speaking from the context of their lives full of sorrow and joy says simply: "It's not all bad."

Infinitesimal specks we human beings may be in the vast scheme of things, caught up in events sometimes too terrible to name, yet there is goodness and hope and reason to believe in each other and tomorrow. There is something that cares and will have its way with us and our world, a force that never gives up seeking us until we at last seek a world where things work like they are supposed to. God is the beginning and end of all life's riddles, in whom we find the answers, if only we have eyes to see.

Gracious God, give us eyes to perceive our place in creation, hearts to know that we are loved and to love one another, wills to respond to your search for our well-being by seeking the well-being of others, and faith to believe that even if tomorrow is uncertain you are not. From the beginning to the end of the human story you spread a table before us in the presence of all our enemies, you are the dwelling place where we shall find serenity. We pray in the name of Jesus Christ who is our perspective. Amen.

Chapter Fourteen

Blessed Are Those Who Defeat Anxiety

Matthew 6:25–33

by Gary E. Parker

You are about to fly on an airplane for the first time. You sit down and strap on your seat belt. You actually *listen* as the attendant describes what to do in the case of emergency. It doesn't help your nerves when she yells you where you can find the exits, how to put on the oxygen mask, and how to use your seat as a floatation device if you crash into the water. She finishes her speech, and you pull a magazine out of the rack, and your eyes land on an article on airplane safety. You read, "Most airplane crashes occur within the first two minutes of take-off." You stare down at your watch. The sweat pours from your armpits and makes half-moons on your shirt.

Tomorrow you will sit down with the personnel manager of a large business firm. You want the job badly. You can use the extra money; you like the location of the opening; you feel excited by the challenge of the promotion. Tonight, though, you can't sleep. You toss and turn, going over and over in your mind what you will say and trying to guess what questions you'll need to answer. The night stretches out longer and longer. You take a deep breath. What happens if you don't get the job? You stare up at the ceiling.

You're sixteen and about to go out on your first single date. You (and I'm telling it from a male perspective) walk to the front door and ring the doorbell. Your hands feel sweaty. Her father answers—and he's big! He ushers you into the den and you take a seat. You look around the room and see the obvious. Your date's dad is a gun collector. He startles you with his deep voice. "Where are you taking my daughter and what time will you have her home?" You speak out a hesitant answer as the sweat rolls off your chin.

These images show us pictures of anxiety. They show us normal people worrying through normal events. All of us suffer at times from anxiety. We expect it to happen. But, if we're not careful, anxiety will squeeze our hearts, choke our voices, and steal away our joy. Anxiety (or "worry" as we often call it) can imprison us, entrap us, and destroy us. Worry can defeat our happiness and upset our inner contentment with life quicker than any other emotional enemy.

Jesus understood the danger of anxiety. Out text offers us his encouragement to lay aside the burdens of worry in exchange for the freedom of faith.

Jesus said, "Do not be anxious about your life." These words, spoken as a part of what we call the Sermon on the Mount, help form a kind of Magna Carta for the fulfilled Christian life. As Part of Jesus' counsel for "Blessedness," this advice flows from his words related to personal relationships, prayer and fasting, and storing up treasures in heaven. Jesus offers us help for discovering genuine happiness, and part of that help includes an encouragement to give up anxiety.

Jesus spoke these words because people of the biblical era worried as much as we do. Jesus spoke specifically to people concerned with the basics of life. The weren't wealthy people concerned about low interest rates on their IRA's. They were poor people wandering about for food and clothing and shelter. They were scared people, fighting to maintain their faith in a hostile world. They were simple people of all circumstances with typical human pressures.

Then, just as now, anxiety threatened to destroy the happiness of life. They had taxes due on the fifteenth; they had elderly mothers who were ill and needed special care; they had projects at work which were behind schedule; they had receding hairlines and expanding belt lines and unsightly age lines. Anxiety was a force which enslaved them, crushed them, and imprisoned them to shut them off from fulfillment.

Not much has changed in two thousand years. We live in an anxious age. We worry a lot. Sixty million valium prescriptions are written every year in The United States. In a recent survey eighty percent of respondents said they suffered from anxiety and were not happy. Over 27,000 suicides will occur in the United States in 1992. These statistics only scratch the surface of the normal, day to day, anxieties we face. We worry about what we've done in the past and about what we didn't do in the past. We worry about what we want to do in the future and about what we can't do in the future. We worry about what we should do and say and what we shouldn't do and say. We worry about children, about parents, about spouses, and friends. If we can't find something to worry about, we worry about our lack of worry! Bound up in our straight jackets of anxiety, we find ourselves unable to reach out and grasp the blessedness Jesus offered to us.

Jesus, though, advised us to let go of our anxiety. He did so because he knew that we can't enjoy the peace of God if we're awash in the anxiety of the soul. We really can't find joy and peace without giving up anxiety. They don't match on the same team. Joy and peace don't fit with worry. They repel each other, like positive and negative poles. When you see worry, you won't see joy and peace, and vice versa. Anxiety defeats joy and peace.

Though Jesus counseled us to give up anxiety, we know that saying it doesn't make it happen. We know it takes more than a word to wipe away worry. What does it take? How can we defeat anxiety and discover happiness?

I could offer scores of techniques to help you do this. The shelves of bookstores are stacked with "how-to" manuals on relieving anxiety. One will advise more exercise, better food, and more sleep. Another will offer counseling therapies, with groups or personal psychologists. A third will discuss relaxation techniques, self-talk and mood tapes. You can use these methods and many of them will help.

My purpose, though, isn't to offer you a modern method to defeat anxiety. Nor can I speak to the deep psychological trauma of panic attacks and other anxiety-produced illnesses. I can't do justice to the worst of anxieties in one sermon. But, we can gain insight into the philosophy of anxiety management. I want to offer you a scripturally based understanding of worrisome ways. By knowing the nature of anxiety, we can better learn to defeat it. To help us do this, I want to share two truths about worry. Then, I want to conclude with one truth about God.

Jesus offered us the initial truth about worry in verse 27. He said, "Which of you by being anxious can add one cubit to his span of life?" Translated, Jesus said, "Worry can't change anything!" Worry won't help you live longer. It won't make you taller. It won't make you richer, or better looking, or healthier, or more successful. Give up worry because you gain absolutely nothing by clutching to it. *We begin to defeat anxiety when we understand the uselessness of it.*

Last winter I bought myself an exercise bicycle. It has rotatable bars so I can pull with my arms at the same time I push with my legs. I sat it behind the sofa downstairs and planned to use it while I watched the news in the evenings. And, occasionally, I do ride it. But, let me tell you—I hate every minute of it! I hate it not because it takes work, but because no matter how hard I pedal, I get nowhere! Fast or slow, it doesn't matter. I'm in the same place when I finish as when I started. Only now I'm tired and sweaty to boot.

Worry works like my bicycle. We pedal and pedal, but it takes us nowhere. It leaves us tired and unhappy, but offers no hope of contentment.

I like the way one man said it—"Worry is like riding a merry-go-round. You pay good money to get on, go round and round, then get off exactly where you started."

To defeat anxiety, see not only the uselessness of it, but also the *faithlessness* of it. Ultimately, we worry because we are afraid. We're afraid of failure. We're afraid of the unknown. We're afraid of danger. We don't feel confident enough in the outcome of the situation. We don't trust something or someone. We don't trust ourselves. We don't trust another person. Or, we don't trust God.

In verse 30, Jesus spoke specifically to this issue. He spoke of those who live in the clutches of anxiety and called them "You of little faith."

The appellation stares back at us. Once we place our cares, our needs, our hurts, and our fears in God's hands we can release the fear from ours. When we trust God enough to give our anxieties to him, we will no longer lose our happiness. The instant we practice enough faith in God to handle our worries, we again the peace of God which surpasses our understanding.

An illiterate farmer had a train to catch early one morning. The train would take him to his son's college graduation. Since the farmer had never had the opportunity to gain an education, he desperately wanted to see his boy accept his diploma. The farmer, who had awakened at the first crack of light every morning for over thirty years, was nervous about missing his train. He feared he would oversleep. To prevent this possibility, he ordered an expensive alarm clock through the Sears and Roebuck catalog. He fretted for the two weeks it took for the clock to arrive. Finally it came, three days before the graduation. The farmer kept the clock wrapped, afraid to use it and wear it out before the big day. The night before graduation arrived. The farmer carefully removed the clock from the package, wound it up, sat it beside his bed, listened to its tick-tock, and watched its face glow in the dark. As he stretched out upon his bed to sleep, he discovered he could not. Concerned the clock wouldn't ring, he stayed up all night to make sure it did. The farmer didn't trust the clock to do what it had been guaranteed to do. His worry prevented his trust. And his lack of trust created his anxiety.

Our anxiety often demonstrates an unfaithful, distrustful relationship with ourselves, with others, and even with God. When we don't have faith in life, we lose the joy and peace of life.

How, then, do we defeat anxiety in life? By understanding it better. By admitting its uselessness. By confessing its faithlessness. But, what else? *Listen* to Jesus. He doesn't tell us to begin an exercise program to release stress and tension; he doesn't advise us to practice better time management and organizational techniques so we can relieve worry by prior planning; he doesn't admonish us to join a group therapy session so we can verbalize our frustration and problems. Though each of these has value, they are not what Jesus suggests.

Speaking of God's care for us in comparison to the birds of the air and the lilies of the field, Jesus asked, "Are you not of more value than they?" and "Will God not so much more clothe you?" Then, Jesus concluded, "Your heavenly father knows you need all these things."

How do we defeat anxiety to find happiness? We defeat it by seeing the uselessness of worry and by confessing the faithlessness of worry. *Ultimately, though, we defeat anxiety only by believing in the trustworthiness of God.* "God," said Jesus, "knows of your cares and needs." "God," said Jesus, "places more value on you in your imperfections than he does even on the birds with their beauty." Be not anxious because the eternal God of the universe, the almighty creator of wind and rain and mountain and waterfall, the God of the night sky and morning dawn—this God knows you personally and cares for you. Here we find the antidote for anxiety. We live in the arms of a personal God who invests the divine life in the human experience. We rest in the security of a loving God who knows us by name and offers us his presence. We depend on a God who takes joy in relating individually to us.

A scientist once suggested a way to understand the immensity of the universe. Imagine a glass pavement, he said. Then shrink our sun from 865,000 miles in diameter to a ball only two feet across. Next. place the ball on the pavement to represent the sun. Step off 82 paces (about two feet per pace) to represent proportionately the first planet, Mercury. Now, put down a tiny mustard seed. Take 60 more steps and drop an ordinary BB on the highway to represent Venus. Mark 78 more steps and place a green pea representing Earth on the clear highway. Step off 108 paces from there, and for Mars put down a pinhead. Sprinkle around some fine dust for the asteroids, then take 788 more steps. For Jupiter, place an orange on the glass pavement. After 934 more steps, drop down a golf ball for Saturn.

(Now it really becomes involved.) Mark 2,086 more steps and set a marble on the highway to represent Uranus. Another 2,322 steps from there and you arrive at Neptune. Let a cherry stand for Neptune. This will take two and a half miles, and we haven't even discussed Pluto! If you swing completely around, you have a smooth glass surface five miles in diameter, representing a tiny fraction of the heavens—excluding Pluto.

On the surface, five miles across, we have only a seed, BB, pea, pinhead, some dust, an orange, a golf ball, a marble, and a cherry. Guess how far you would have to go on the same scale before you could put down another two-foot thick ball to represent the nearest star! Seven hundred paces? Two thousand more steps? Four thousand four hundred feet? No, much more! You'd have to go 6,720 *miles* before you could arrive at that star. And that's just the first star among millions. In one galaxy among perhaps thousands, maybe billions.[1]

And Jesus said that God, in the midst of such immensity, cares for us, individually. What a relief! We're not alone. In all our fears, problems, and worries, we're not alone.

At times our anxieties threaten to over whelm us. But, fear not!. God cares for each of us. Be not anxious, for God knows you by Name. Blessed are those who allow God to overcome their anxieties with his holy presence. Amen.

Notes

[1]This illustration is taken from Charles R. Swindoll, *Come Before Winter*, (Portland, OR: Multnomah Press, 1985), 295–296.

Chapter Fifteen

Giving Up Our Judgeship

Matthew 7:1-5

by Johnny F. McKinney

"Do not judge!" It is almost impossible to avoid, isn't it? Judging seems to run in our blood. We meet people and immediately size them up. We weigh them on our scales, evaluate them, pigeonhole them. This business of judging is never very far from our minds. As someone once observed, "Most of us are umpires at heart; we like to call balls and strikes on somebody else."

Our bent toward passing judgement causes us to look beyond the person and assign them to their group or niche. Individuals become "red-necks," "poor trash," "yuppies," "rich tyrants," "religious freaks," "young radicals," "old fogies," "do-gooders," "trash," "tramps," "conservatives," "liberals," "worthless," "lazy." There is no end to our list of categories. Not only do we do it, we enjoy doing it. No doubt it gives us some feeling of superiority.

All the while we fear being on the receiving end of other people's judgement of us. We worry about public opinion. We worry about the judgement of our neighbors more than we worry about final judgement.

"Do not judge!" I am convinced that this is one of the most difficult standards Jesus set for his followers. It certainly ranks right up there with "Love your enemies," "Go the second mile," and "In everything, do to others what you would have them do to you." Jesus knows our hearts well. He knows our temptation to treat other people as things rather than human beings. Jesus had been on the receiving end of such judgements. He experienced the destructive power of being labeled, written off, because of his association with "tax-collectors and sinners."

Does that mean that all judging is unbecoming and harmful? Naturally, it depends on your definition of judging. Jesus was not insinuating that we should avoid making decisions, determinations, and evaluations. He was not asking that discriminating appraisals or concern for worthy conduct be ignored. Jesus was not implying that we should have no opinion regarding what is right or wrong, that we have no moral discernment. He was not suggesting that we not care for other people.

Jesus is warning against censorship of other persons. He is opposing the judgmental spirit which condemns others, criticizes others and censors others without mercy or compassion. We are to remember that the same standard we use to judge others will be used to judge us; "measure for measure" says Jesus. There are three implications in Jesus' words about judgement.

Our judgement of others is *IRRESPONSIBLE.* We are not God,nor are we to put ourselves in the position of God. As George Buttrick observes, ". . . man's role is not that of judge. That is to say, the whole business is a perversion and denial of human nature."[1] The writer of James drives home the point: "There is only one lawgiver and judge, the one who is able to save and destroy. But you—who are you to judge your neighbor?" (4:12)

My judgment is irresponsible because of my limited 0perspective. Jesus paints the ludicrous picture of a man with a plank in his own eye attempting to assist the brother with a speck of sawdust in his eye. Our censorious judgement of others is just as ridiculous.

One of the best commentaries on this thought is a "Peanuts" cartoon. Little Linus, looking forlorn and weary asks Lucy, "Why are you always so anxious to criticize me?" Lucy, with all the confidence her self-righteous mood could muster responds, "I just think I have a knack for seeing other people's faults." Linus indignantly snaps, "What about your own faults." "I have a knack for overlooking them," says Lucy.

My knowledge of others is limited and I am forced to judge on the basis of externals; I don't know their hearts. It is so easy to draw unwarranted conclusions that are not easily replaced by the truth. Some of life's embarrassing moments occur when we are too quick to judge.

The story is told of a young American who attended a banquet, at which he found himself seated next to a Chinese diplomat. Not knowing what to say to a Chinese, the young man ask, "Likee soupee?" The Chinese diplomat merely nodded and smiled politely. Later during the banquet, the diplomat, Wellington Koo, was called on to speak and delivered an eloquent address in flawless English. As he sat down to the applause of the crowd, he turned to the young American and asked "Likee speechee?"[2] The scriptures warn us against assuming the role of judge because of our limited perspectives. Indeed, " . . . God sees not as man sees, for man looks at the outward appearance, but the Lord looks at the heart" (1 Sam 16:7).

Not only is my perspective limited, but my own sinfulness gets in the way of my judging others. As Shakespeare notes through his character in *Henry VI*, "Forbear to judge, for we are sinners all." Nowhere does this become more apparent than in Jesus' encounter with the woman caught in the act of adultery in John 8. The broken woman was deposited at Jesus' feet and her accusers demanded a verdict, based on the Law of Moses. Jesus does not condone her act, but he chooses to deal with the attitude of her would-be judges. "If any one of you is without sin, let him be the first to throw a stone at her" (John 8:7). That is the heart of the matter when it comes to our judging others. We are all sinners, and sinners cannnot be stone-throwers. In the words of Thomas à Kempis, "He that well and rightly considereth his own works will find little cause to judge hardly of another."

My judgement of others is also irresponsible because my motives are less than pure. Why do I judge so quickly? Is it in judging others I take my mind off my own sins? There is a self-righteous motive. I make myself look better if I compare myself with the weaknesses and faults of others. Perhaps I take comfort in someone else's faults because "misery loves company." Or maybe I judge others so readily because I am jealous; in my heart I would like to be committing the same sins I condemn. A British psychiatrist, Dr. J. A. Hadfield put the matter this way:

> In judging others we trumpet abroad our secret faults. We personalize our unrecognized failings, and hate in others the very faults to which we are secretly addicted. Like the lark fluttering with agitation over her nest, we exhibit most flagrantly the very thing we would hide.[3]

If we choose to judge another, to take measure of their lives, we have set the standard by which we shall be judged. "Measure for measure," says Jesus. It is easy to see that grace and mercy must become our guidelines.

God has not given us the final word on our fellow human beings. We should not assume the role. Buttrick reminds us,

> This earth is not a law court, and we are not God's prosecuting attorneys. We are not good enough by a long shot, and we do not know enough about God's deeper laws, and the man in the dock would in any case be our brother.[4]

Our judgment of others is irresponsible, but there is a second implication in this warning of Jesus.

Others' judgement of us is IRRELEVANT. I do not have the last word on other people, nor do they have the last word on me. The judgement of others becomes inconsequential and immaterial. I can still live effectively in the presence of my judges. Jesus says, "Do not judge!"

Lewis Smedes has an interesting chapter in one of his books titled: "The Gift of Freedom: All The World's a Critic, and You're Tired of Reading the Reviews." In that chapter he observes:

> One of the fine arts of gracious living is the art of living freely with our critics. When we have the grace to be free in the presence of those who judge our lives and evaluate our actions, we have Christian freedom.[5]

Until we realize this we are likely to be pawns in the hands of public opinion and to fall into the trap of false prophets in the Old Testament who chose to be "pleasers of men" rather than "pleasers of God." It is correct to say that in earlier generations what people feared most was "falling into the hands of an angry God." Today we are more concerned about the opinions of our contemporaries. H. G. Wells summarized it well when he said, "The voice of our neighbor speaks more loudly to us than does the voice of God."

We easily become confined to living out our lives in the arena of other people's opinions and become slaves to peer pressure and jump on any band-wagon that comes along. We are tempted to settle for finding our meaning in life in the estimations of others and take our signals from their whims and ideas. It is possible to become sick trying to please other people. Psychologists call such tangled relationships "co-dependency."

The apostle Paul understood the implications of Jesus' teaching about human judgement. He offered a Christian declaration of independence when he wrote:

I care very little if I am judged by you or by any human court; indeed, I do not even judge myself. My conscience is clear, but that does not make me innocent. It is the Lord who judges me. Therefore judge nothing before the appointed time; wait till the Lord comes. He will bring to light what is hidden in darkness and will expose the motives of men's hearts. At that time each will receive his praise from God (1 Cor 4:3-5).

Paul had his share of critics, but he did not allow that to cripple him. At the time Paul was being brutalized by critics in Corinth, but that had always been the story of his life. Had he listened to all of his judges he would have thrown in the towel on being an apostle. Some said he was too short and ugly to be an apostle and others said his poor eyesight really made him ineffective. Besides that, they complained, "Paul is really not an effective public speaker." Some said he was too conservative; others said he was too liberal. Some said he made things too simple; others argued he made them too complex. Some said Paul was too concerned about the Gentiles; others asserted that he had not moved far enough away from his Jewish roots. Some said he didn't exercise enough control over the churches he helped establish; others charged that he was too authoritarian.

Paul could never get away from his critics, but he did manage to put things in proper perspective. "I care very little if I am judged by you or by any human court." "Your opinion of me is not the final verdict." Paul knew that mankind is not qualified to act as his brother's judge. He had to follow his own convictions and march to his own drum beat. Paul would not be condemned by the high court of human opinion. It would not rob him of his peace or productivity.

Lewis Smedes tells of a young woman he met who had lived out her life as a slave of other people's opinions. She was a beautiful woman who was about fifty years old. She was bright, talented, and well-educated and looked as though she had just stepped off the pages of *Vogue*. She had just attempted suicide. At age fifty she realized she had lived her entire life only to please other people. She was always afraid she would disappoint them, be criticized by them, and somehow not measure up. She reached fifty and perceived that she had lived for a half-century in the prison of other people's opinions.[6]

Many of us find ourselves in just such a predicament. This woman's story resembles so many of our stories. All of this is not to say that public opinion has no role, or that other's evaluation of us is of no value. It is a call to put things in proper perspective. Whom do we seek to please? Whose opinion matters most to us? Whom do we live our lives for?

In the end, the judgement of others is not the last word on my life. I ultimately seek to please God. And that brings me to the final implication of Matthew 7:1-6.

God's judgment of us is *IRREVOCABLE*. God has the final say on our lives. Jesus says "you will be judged." We do not avoid judgment by refraining from judging others, we merely change the standard of measurement. We are ultimately answerable to God.

Perhaps that in itself is an uncomfortable assertion to us moderners. We think of ourselves as the final arbiters, the ultimate judges of life. But not so, according to the New Testament. "This will take place on the day when God will judge men's secrets through Jesus Christ," attests Paul. (Rom 2:16) That being the case, God becomes our most important audience and his opinion is one we cannot overlook. As Paul again affirms, "So we make it our goal to please him, whether we are at home in the body or away from it, for we must all appear before the judgment seat of Christ, that each one may receive what is due him." (2 Cor 5:9-10) That being the case the will of God becomes the guideline for your life, not popular opinion or even tuggings of conscience.

Life takes on meaning in light of judgment. If there are no boundaries, no goals, no destinations life is purposeless and both God and the universe are not fair. There may be little distinction now between the results of good and evil, but that is not an argument against God's final say.

Charles Allen tells of a farmer who once wrote the editor of a newspaper:

> Dear Mr. Editor: My neighbor goes to church and observes Sunday. I ploughed my fields on Sunday. I sowed my fields on Sunday. I harvested on Sunday. Mr. Editor, at the end of the season and the end of the harvest, I did better than any of my neighbors who observed Sunday and went to church. How do you explain that?

The editor's answer was brief. He wrote: "God doesn't make up His final account in October."[8]

Some graphic pictures of judgement in past generations have no doubt been based on sensationalism and perhaps a secret desire to give others what they deserve. We cannot allow the extremism of the past to distort our current perspective. The message of the early church is still relevant: "And He ordered us to preach to the people, and solemnly to testify that this is the one who has been appointed by God as judge of the living and the dead." (Acts 10:42)

The redeeming word for us in all of this is that the God who judges us is the God who loves us. The Christ we encounter at the judgement is the same Christ we encounter at the cross, dying for our sins. This changes our entire understanding of judgment. "In this way, love is made complete amongst so that we will have confidence on the day of judgment, because in this world we are like him. There is no fear in love. But perfect love drives out fear." (I John 4:17ff)

As Frederick Buechner observes:

> The New Testament proclaims that at some unforeseeable time in the future God will ring down the final curtain on history, and there will come a Day on which all our days and all the judgments upon us and all our judgments upon each other will themselves be judged. The judge will be

Christ. In other words, the one who judges us most finally
will be the one who loves us most fully. [8]

Thank God for his love. The matchless love we have encountered in Christ at the cross gives us confidence for judgment.
May it also keep us from judging our neighbors and from being prisoners of their judgments.
    What freedom! Freedom from the need to judge. Freedom
to live before my critics. Freedom to try to please God!

Notes

[1]George A. Buttrick, *Sermons Preached In A University Church* (Nashville: Abingdon Press, 1959) 119.

[2] "Judging--Sometime Premature," *Preaching* 3 (1987): 49.

[3]J. A. Davidson, "Sitting In Judgment on the Other Person," *Pulpit
Digest* 63 (1983): 359.

[4]Buttrick 121–22.

[5]Lewis B. Smedes, *How Can Everything Be All Right When Everything
Is All Wrong?* (San Francisco: Harper & Row, 1982) 37.

[6] Ibid., 40–41.

[7]Charles L. Allen, *The Sermon On The Mount* (New Jersey: Fleming H.
Revell Company, 1966) 149.

[8]Frederick Buechner, *Wishful Thinking: A Theological ABC* (New York:
Harper & Row, 1973) 48.

Chapter Sixteen

The Biggest Lie

Matthew 7:24–29

by Scott Nash

Lying is such a pervasive part of our common existence that we have come to expect it in certain quarters.

We expect it in politics. In the thick of political campaigns, lying has proved to be an effective tool. Half-truths, innuendos, insinuations, and outright fabrications are the adopted means for undermining one's opponent or presenting oneself as someone he or she is not. The outrageous scandals of national administrations during the past three decades have almost de-sensitized us to the severity of ongoing betrayals of the national trust. We assume that such behavior is a normal part of government. When one former president first accepted his party's nomination for the office and asserted that he would never lie to the American people, his words were met with skepticism and disbelief. Many have come to believe that most, if not all, politicians are charter members of the liar's club.

We expect the same in business, especially in the realm of advertisement. We know that those well-groomed, articulate persons who share their glowing testimonies about the merits of a particular product are simply actors being paid to recite their scripts. We know that the product freshly re-packaged and promoted as "new and improved" is really the same old stuff. We know that such claims as "We do it all for you" could actually be translated as "We do it all for profit." We know better than to take such claims seriously.

We expect the same in crime. We've learned to say sarcastically that there are no guilty people behind bars —they all claim innocence of the crimes charged against them. We have come to expect indictments for criminal activity to be countered with pleas of "not guilty" on the basis of entrapment, temporary insanity, political motivation, or plain ignorance of the law. We may even think of how refreshing it would be to see those caught "red-handed" in a crime confess their responsibility and guilt rather than appeal to extenuating circumstances or hide behind a maze of constitutional complexities in a prolonged and expensive process of litigation. We even relish in telling jokes about the legal profession, chiding those lawyers who enjoy the profits of a what we perceive to be a process that distorts the truth.

The pervasiveness of lying in our society has come to be accepted by many as a fact of life. We may decry the prominence of lying, but too often we resign ourselves to it as an inevitable part of the way the system works, even succumbing to the effectiveness of its tactics and indulging in a little twisting of facts for our own benefit. In all of this, truth takes a beating.

Religion is not immune to the prevalence of lying. Scandals have rocked the electronic church. Denominational factions have played loose with the facts. Even local churches have felt the pain of deception within its ranks. From at least one perspective, the modern church may be the arena in which the greatest lie of all is being propagated. In fact, the biggest lie being told in America today may just be the assertion that Jesus Christ is Lord.

At least that is the charge that Clarence Jordan once made to a group of church leaders.[1] Jordan asked those assembled to consider the degree of loyalty among their church members to Jesus and his teachings. He asked them to estimate the percentage of their members who, if faced with a fundamental choice between obeying the teachings of Jesus and obeying the dictates of custom, money, or the law, would choose to obey Jesus. After a period of intense discussion, the church leaders came to a consensus that at most only one or two per cent of their church members would choose to obey Jesus rather than custom, money, or law. Jordan pointed out that what they were in effect saying was that 98 per cent of their church members were liars. They had made a public profession that Jesus Christ was the Lord of their lives and had signified that profession through baptism. But they did not mean it. In effect, they had lied. Therefore, Jordan charged, that means that the biggest lie being told in America today is that *Jesus Christ is Lord*.

Jesus himself acknowledged that persons could profess him as Lord and not really mean it. He brought his Sermon on the Mount to a close with a pair of parables that pointed out the folly of hearing his words and not doing them. "Every one who hears these words of mine and does them," Jesus said, "will be like a wise person who built his or her house upon the rock" (5:24). When the rains fell, the floods came, and the winds blew and beat upon that house, it did not fall because it was founded on the rock. But the reverse also held. "Every one who hears these words of mine and does not do them," he said, "will be like a fool (literally, a "moron," from the Greek word *mōros*) who built his or her house upon the sand" (5:26). When the rains fell, the floods came, and the winds blew and beat against the house, it fell with a tremendous collapse.

The point of Jesus' words is painfully clear. Hearing without doing is a tragic lie. Immediately before these concluding parables, Jesus announced that not everyone who said, "Lord, Lord," would enter into the kingdom (5:21). Only those who actually did the will of the heavenly father would enter. Even those who came prepared to defend their records by boasting of their religious accomplishments would fail to enter. In fact, they would be dismissed as unknowns (5:22–23). Jesus drew a rigid distinction between doing good things and doing the right things—a distinction difficult to draw by those who intend to be good persons but live in a world where the lie is woven into the very fabric of existence. Sorting out the truth as the solid foundation for life is difficult in a land where shifting, sandy ground is the norm.

Jesus emphasized that the "hearing and doing of *these words of mine*" is the challenge that confronts Christians. The phrase "these words" is repeated for special emphasis. Matthew picked up this refrain as he described the conclusion of Jesus' preaching: "And it happened that when Jesus finished *these words*, the crowds were astonished at his teaching, for he was teaching them as one having authority and not as their scribes" (5:28–29). "These words" to which Jesus called for obedience (and Matthew depicted the crowds' astonishment) were the words of the sermon just concluded. Hearing and doing *these words* marked the difference between living according to the truth and living a great lie.

The crowds perceived that *these words* were spoken with unusual authority. The question of authority often arises as we try to sift through the competing claims for truth. Often we acknowledge the authority of Jesus. We may appeal, however, to other authorities for interpretation of *these words* of Jesus. Sometimes authoritative interpreters grant us a way around *these words* of Jesus by transporting them into the realm of impracticability and irrelevance. Sometimes the way around *these words* even comes through appeal to the Bible, itself. Since the Bible is openly recognized (and forcefully defended by some) as the complete authority for all of life's questions, some feel fortunate to find it allows for other interpretations that neutralize the stringency of Jesus' words. The authority of the one who spoke *these words*, then, becomes secondary to other religious authorities.

Speaking to a group of students at a Baptist college, Frank Stagg recently made a case for hearing and doing *these words* of Jesus. For some of those students, most of whom are from very conservative churches, the issue of believing Jesus' words was easily resolved by the fact that they are in the Bible—"God said it; I believe it; that settles it!" Reading his audience well, Stagg asserted, "Of course, I believe it because Jesus said it. But Jesus said it because it's *true*."[2] *These words* of Jesus astonished the crowds and continue to carry the same astounding authority *because* they are true.

Here at the end of the Sermon on the Mount, we can reflect upon *these words* of Jesus and continue to be astonished—because they run so counter to what we know from usual human experience; because they fly in the face of the ways that practice and tradition, even sacred tradition, have hallowed; because they seem to be not of this world; because they represent an ideal to which we would like to aspire but believe that we cannot; because they demand so much of us. But we can also be astonished because *these words* are true.

Remember the Beatitudes that affirm God's good blessing for those who seem to have none of this world's blessings.

Remember that God has made Christians to be salt and light in the world and that they will of necessity function as salt and light if God has made them such.

Remember that there is a greater righteousness that goes beyond that defined and allowed by religious tradition.

Remember that anger, lust, retaliation, and limited love make it impossible for us to experience our humanness in the ways God intended.

Remember that piety, however orthodox or commendably practiced, brings only a limited result and may even stand in the way of true communion with God and neighbor.

Remember that we really cannot serve God and mammon, for divided loyalties produce schizophrenic selves and rob us of a coherent center.

Remember that anxieties about food, drink, and attire really do enslave us to fear over security and keep us from being daringly faithful.

Remember that judging others really does blind us to our own humanity and leads us into complacency.

Remember that God really is for us and can be trusted to provide for what we really need.

Remember that the Golden Rule really is the foundation for genuine human interaction.

Remember that a tree really is known by its fruits, that authentic good cannot be produced by the spirit of self-interest—no matter how righteous the actions produced by that spirit may appear.

Remember that *these words* are true. And remember that those who hear the truth of *these words* but content themselves with living by other words are, themselves, participating in the biggest lie.

When Clarence Jordan—who labored to build a genuine Christian community upon the rock of *these words* of truth —had shocked his audience with his charge that 98 per cent of all church members were living a lie, he then reminded the group of these closing parables in Jesus' great sermon. The *wise* build their lives on the rock of Jesus and his teachings. But the *idiots*, hearing these words and failing to do them, build their houses on the sands that cannot support them against the chaos of deceit. "Let us go forth," Jordan said, "and classify ourselves."[3]

And so we shall.

Notes

[1]From an audio tape of selected messages by Jordan entitled *Clarence Jordan—Man of Faith* (Americus, GA: Koinonia Partners, 1992).

[2]From comments made during the Horton Lectures at Brewton-Parker College, October 27, 1992.

[3]Jordan apparently coined the term "idiot" for translation here. He makes a similar statement about classifying ourselves in *Sermon on the Mount*, rev. ed. (Valley Forge, PA: Judson Press, 1952.

Biographical Notes

David C. Crocker is pastor of Central Baptist Church, Johnson City, Tennessee. A graduate of Belmont College (B.A.), and The Southern Baptist Theological Seminary (M.Div.; D.Min.), he has served churches in Alabama, Kentucky, Indiana, and Tennessee. He has produced several church-oriented publications and has served on the Executive Board of the Tennessee Baptist Convention.

William E. Flippin is pastor of Greater Piney Grove Baptist Church, Atlanta, Georgia. He was the associate director of the Department of Black Church Relations for the Georgia Baptist Convention 1982–90 and became that state convention's Black Church consultant in 1990. A graduate of Fisk University (B.A.), Candler School of Theology of Emory University (M.Div.), and McCormick Theological Seminary (D.Min.). Dr. Flippin has been active in National Baptist Convention educational activities and was appointed to the Governor's Commission on Children and Youth in Georgia.

Thomas H. Graves is the president of Baptist Theological Seminary at Richmond.He is a graduate of Vanderbilt University, The Southern Baptist Theological Seminary, and Yale Divinity School. he has taught at Bellarmine College, Barton College, Southern Seminary, Palm Beach Atlantic College, and Southeastern Baptist Theological Seminary. The author of numerous publications, he has been a campus minister and pastor of churches in Kentucky, Florida, and North Carolina.

David B. Howell is currently Assistant Professor of Religion at Carson-Newman College in Jefferson City, Tennessee. Previously, he was the Senior Associate Dean of Students and Adjunct Instructor in Religion at William Jewell College. David has degrees from William Jewell College (A.B.), Southeastern Baptist Theological Seminary (M.Div., Th.M.), and the University of Oxford (D.Phil.). He is the author of one book on Matthew entitled *Matthew's Inclusive Story* (1990).

J. Estill Jones was Seminary Pastor for The Southern Baptist Theological Seminary 1983–91. A graduate of Oklahoma Baptist University (A.B.) and Southern Seminary (Th.M.; Th.D.), he taught at Southern Seminary (1946–51) and Midwestern Baptist Seminary (occasionally 1973–82). Dr. Jones has been the pastor of churches in Kentucky and Georgia. he has also been a consultant for various denominational agencies and has been a frequent speaker for conferences and retreats. He has written numerous articles and books. He and his wife have now retired to Chatsworth, Georgia.

Clarence Jordan was the founder of Koinonia Partners near Americus, Georgia. He was noted as a preacher, Greek New Testament scholar and translator, author, and prophetic social activist. He received a B.S. in agriculture from the University of Georgia and the Th.M. and Ph.D. degrees from The Southern Baptist Theological Seminary. He died in 1969.

Linda E. Jordan is the Senior Minister of the Olin T. Binkley Memorial Baptist Church in Chapel Hill, North Carolina. She has been a campus minister and a military chaplain, as well as serving Southern Baptist, American Baptist, and Presbyterian churches in Mississippi, South Carolina, and North Carolina. Dr. Jordan is a graduate of Furman University (B.A.), The Southern Baptist Theological Seminary (M.Div.), and San Francisco Theological Seminary (D. Min.).

J. Mark Lawson, a native of Arkansas, holds the M.Div. and Ph.D. degrees from The Southern Baptist Theological Seminary. He has served churches in Arkansas, Kentucky, Indiana, and Germany, and is now pastor of Bellewood Baptist Church (SBC), North Syracuse, New York.

Johnny F. McKinney is pastor of First Baptist Church, Gaffney, South Carolina. He is a graduate of Milligan College (B.A.) and The Southern Baptist Theological Seminary (M.Div.; D.Min.). Pastor of churches in Kentucky, Tennessee, and South Carolina, he has also been an adjunct professor of religion at Gardner-Webb College. He was included in the 4th edition of *Who's Who in Religion.*

Scott Nash is senior editor for books for Smyth & Helwys Publishing, Inc., managing editor for Mercer University Press, and adjunct associate professor of Christianity at Mercer University. For eight years he was the Barney Averitt Chair of Christianity and Chairman of the Division of Religious and Philosophical studies at Brewton-Parker College. A graduate of the Centre College of Kentucky (B.A.) and The Southern Baptist Theological Seminary (M.Div.; Ph.D.), he has been the pastor of churches in Kentucky and Georgia.

Gary E. Parker is pastor of First Baptist Church, Jefferson City, Missouri. Previous pastorates include churches in North Carolina, South Carolina, and Texas. He is a graduate of Furman University (B.A.), Southeastern Baptist Theological Seminary (M.Div.), and Baylor University (Ph.D.). He is the author of several articles and four books, including *Principles Worth Protecting* published by Smyth & Helwys.

Carole Harvey ("Kate") Penfield is minister of the First Baptist Church in America, Providence, Rhode Island. The mother of a daughter and four sons, she has been a high school french teacher, employment counselor, chaplain, religion instructor, and pastor. She is a graduate of the State University of New York at Albany (B.A.), University of Cincinnati (M.Ed.), and Andover-Newton Theological School (M.Div.), she has been active in denominational affairs of the American Baptists Churches USA, including editing the denominational publication, *The Minister.*

T. C. Smith is professor emeritus of Furman University. A graduate of Louisiana College, The Southern Baptist Theological Seminary, and the University of Edinburgh, Dr. Smith has taught at several schools, including Southern Seminary, Southeastern Baptist Theological Seminary, Berkeley Baptist Divinity School, and the American University of Beirut. He has served churches in Virginia and North Carolina. Dr. Smith is the author of two books published by Smyth & Helwys: *Studies in Acts* (1991) and *The Sermon on the Mount. A Study Guide* (1992).

Frank Stagg is professor emeritus of The Southern Baptist Theological Seminary where he was for many years the James Buchanan Harrison Professor of New Testament Interpretation. A graduate of Louisiana College (B.A.) and Southern Seminary (Th.M.; Ph.D.), Dr. Stagg also taught at New Orleans Baptist Theological Seminary and has been the pastor of churches in Louisiana. He has been a prolific writer and numbers among his works the commentary on the Gospel of Matthew in the *Broadman Bible Commentary.*